Millions of M

By anonymous authors who ha
variety of addictions and other
behaviours by using 12-Step programmes ot
recovery.

'My workshop stands on a hill, back of our home. Looking over the valley, I see the village community house where our local group meets. Beyond the circle of my horizon lies the whole world of AA.'

Bill Wilson, founder of Alcoholics Anonymous (AA) wrote this in 1960 when AA was 25 years old. By 2020, AA had given birth to many other 12-Steps of Recovery fellowships in one hundred and seventy-five countries and eighty languages through which millions of men, women, and children have recovered from otherwise fatal illnesses. These range from alcoholism, all forms of drug addiction, food and gambling problems to sex, and almost every type of emotional disorder.

The stories in *Millions of Miracles* highlight the knock-on benefit to their families and societies wherever recovery occurs, and the potential that exists to help the hundreds of millions who still suffer from any of these issues all over the world. Each story is true. The writers share only their personal experience, they do not speak for, or on behalf of the fellowships that helped them achieve sobriety or emotional stability.

Foreword by Tony Adams MBE former Captain of England and Arsenal football teams, and founder of Sporting Chance and SIX Mental Health Solutions for men and women who suffer addiction or mental health issues.

There is a saying you will hear if you go to 12-Step meetings for addicts: if you cannot remember your rock bottom, then you probably have not had it. I remember mine vividly. It was 1996, at the end of seven weeks daily drinking following our loss to Germany in the semi-final of the European football Championships.

With much difficulty, I had managed not to take a drink in the build-up and during the tournament itself. I had crossed the line with my addiction, and knew that if I did take a drink, I would not be in a state to play, never mind Captain my country, England. But I also knew that as soon as the tournament was over, I would hit the booze again. Alcohol had become the unwanted and unwelcome partner in my life. I might have been successful in my professional life as a footballer, but on a personal level I had always felt inadequate and awkward; the drug aspect of alcohol helped me to medicate those feelings.

As I celebrate my 25th year of sobriety, I reflect on what a remarkable life I have had since quitting drinking. I became a different, less aggressive more composed footballer who won the Double of Premier League and FA Cup with Arsenal in 1998 and 2002 and played for England at the World Cup in France. Since retiring in 2002, I have had a coaching career that took me from an FA Cup win with Portsmouth, to Holland, Azerbaijan, China and Spain. Above all, I have become a better human being, less absorbed in my issues, more open to other people and the possibilities in life and the potential within me. Knowing these things, led me to new pastures.

What was freely given to me by new friends who had had similar problems, meant I knew I needed to pass on to others similarly afflicted. So, in 2000 I established the Sporting Chance charity to help sports men and women with addictive illnesses. We developed from providing residential treatment based on the 12-Step programme principles, to offering educational talks in sports clubs and bodies on a nationwide basis. Since then, I have become increasingly proud of the work we have done in turning thousands of lives around.

During lockdown, I received many calls from friends and others who were struggling: isolation and confinement had highlighted serious mental health and/or addiction issues. These were people from industry or the entertainment world rather than sport. As a result, I decided to start a new company, SIX Mental Health Solutions (named after the number on my football shirt), which is also based on the 12-Step recovery programmes. This has taken off, showing how much demand there is for understanding the human condition and recovery from stresses based on principles that work.

Helping others using the principles of 12-Step programmes is what this book is about, and I am happy to support its aims and ambition of throwing light on the pain of active addiction and other emotional issues by showing that there are ways out.

My hope is that the stories it contains will inspire people, the way similar messages of recovery inspired me to conquer my alcohol problem and the many others who have also recovered.

Tony Adams.

FOR THE LOST

To all the broken and the battered,
if your eyes should stumble upon these lines
when hope by storms lies shattered,
know you are not alone.
There is an hour in every heart
where words no longer echo.
They fall,
starving,
upon cold ears.
To you I promise,
you are not alone.
This hour,
this empty, eternal hour,
where peace and life are no longer
the same side of the coin,
this hour is hell.
I know how tired you are – believe me,
I know it well.
I begged for sleep
amidst this un-resting cold, when, beneath the sea
my heart plunged like stone,
there appeared night-watchmen
carrying stars,
to light the long way home.

Jaz Dalrymple

First Author's Preface

My name is Jack and I am a former alcoholic and drug addict. Since I began writing *Millions of Miracles* five years ago, more than twelve million people have died from alcoholism and drug addiction; many of which should have been prevented.

As a recovered alcoholic and drug addict, I am a passionate advocate of Alcoholics Anonymous and Narcotics Anonymous's 12-Step programme that saved my life. Since I got sober in 1985 I have directly witnessed hundreds of thousands of former alcoholics, drug addicts, and sufferers of many forms of emotional disorders in thirty-four countries on five continents who have recovered from their problems by following the principles of this simple programme. Today, this success runs into three and a half million.

My hope, and that of the other writers of this book, is that the message first established by AA in 1935, then NA in 1953, be passed on to as many people as possible around the world who suffer emotional disorders and all forms of addiction. Because, if these programmes had been given the support they deserved by politicians and the medical profession, many of the 150 million plus men, women and children who died from the diseases of drug addiction and alcoholism since 1935 would not have done so.

Each man and woman's story in *Millions of Miracles* is fact and based on that individuals experience.

Where opinions are expressed by me, they are based on my past experience as an alcoholic and drug addict, time in recovery using the AA and NA 12-Step programmes, thirty years as a consultant to the pharmaceutical industry and a previous occupation as a British police officer.

I have never blamed the brewing industry for my alcoholism nor pharmaceutical firms for my addiction to their drugs, though they could do much more to advise the public of the dangers there are to using them. Nor did I blame the doctors and psychiatrists who prescribed the tranquillisers and sleeping pills that led to my descent into drug addiction, because at that time (1960 - 85) little was known about their dangerous side-effects with regard to addiction.

Today, in spite of what is overwhelming evidence to the contrary, prescription drug substitution is still the most commonly used treatment to tackle alcoholism, heroin, cocaine, crack, cannabis, LSD, ecstasy and gambling addictions, food and emotional disorders and depression.

As my experience of addiction and recovery is much the same as that of millions of others all over the world where this policy failed, including the millions prescribed opiates and anti-depressants, many more will die unless radical changes are made to the world's drug laws and how the medical profession treats addiction; both of which are hugely influenced by the pharmaceutical industry and politics.

As well as preventing the deaths of the many who died, this approach led to their families and societies suffering needlessly, because it was not made clear to the afflicted there was a freely available solution that could save their lives and prevent the social and criminal mayhem this caused.

Early in my recovery I realised I had unwittingly come face to face with the absurdity of the world's drug laws as they applied to legal and illegal drugs. I spoke about it to my counsellor and the psychiatrists treating me, but because of the fragility of my mind at the time they advised me that it was best if I keep off this subject, just to remember that for addicts like me *all* addictive drugs are poison and if I was to take any I would be threatening my life.

Since then, far too often I have read about someone famous who died of a drug and/or alcohol overdose. Though this is always sad, and makes headline news about the horrors of addiction, these deaths distort the truth; the millions of others who died the same way are never mentioned except as part of the statistics.

With the facts known today, this should not happen, but it does. It is often because those in the medical profession need to be better informed – especially in non-English-speaking countries. Much of the problem seems to be caused by it not being in the financial interests of Big Pharma to expose the truth about the global success of AA and NA as they promote their products instead.

This has meant neither AA nor NA has become well established in most countries, and in some they do not exist at all, so countless lives are lost unnecessarily. As these may have included your mother or father, son or daughter, husband or wife, brother or sister, it is time everyone knows the truth. Otherwise only you and the statisticians will ever know.

As I came to understand these facts, I knew I had an obligation to share my experience and let the world's mothers and fathers be the judges and demand changes if they deem it right. After reading *Millions of Miracles* I hope they reach the same conclusion as me. This could mean that the solution that was freely given to the 3,500,000 who have recovered to date, is made available to every alcoholic and drug addict in the world today.

The chapters of this book tell the recovery stories of former alcoholics and addicts to many classifications of addiction. By doing so, it is hoped the pharmaceutical and brewing firms that make many of the drugs, and the world's governments that support current drug laws, review their positions and work together to make the changes which are exposed that will save millions of lives.

The aim of writing *Millions of Miracles* is to:

1. Make available to every addict in every country in the world a solution to their disease which, when applied, results in permanent recovery from all mood-altering addictive drugs.

2. Put pressure on the World Health Organisation and United Nations to:

a.   Admit alcoholism, drug addiction and addictions are diseases.

b.   Admit the established medical facts about recovery from addiction recovery: that overall drug substitution does not work, only permanent abstinence does.

c.   Advise the medical profession in every country that there are   available, proven, free programmes that can provide recovery from addiction.

3. Put pressure on governments, law makers, pharmaceutical, alcohol and gambling firms, the WHO and UN to admit the 'war on drugs' has caused immense harm to society and families by preventing many addicts' recovering.

4. Inform the public of the truth about addictive drugs, dependency, and addiction, thereby reducing the present stigma attached to alcoholism and drug addiction, which is a major obstacle to recovery, especially in Muslim countries.

5. Put pressure on politicians to change the drug laws that compound the problem.

6. Put forward a workable solution to rectify the situation.

Part 1

Introduction

Over the last few years, many well-known men and women have died as a result of the effects of alcohol and drug abuse. These include Robin Williams, Philip Seymour Hoffman, Heath Ledger, George Best, Whitney Houston, Amy Winehouse, Peaches Geldof, Charles Kennedy, Michael Jackson and Prince.

Before then superstars such as Elvis Presley, Richard Burton, Janis Joplin, Jimi Hendrix, Keith Moon, Howard Hughes, Marilyn Monroe, Raymond Chandler, Sigmund Freud, Dylan Thomas, and Scott Fitzgerald suffered the same fate.

As these famous people represent a miniscule percentage of the total number of addicts and alcoholics who have died during this time, they are unrepresentative of reality. The shocking truth is that the overall number who perished this way is millions, and tragically a huge number of these deaths – including those named above – were caused by misinformation and addiction to *legal drugs*.

For a growing number of years more and more medical professionals and politicians have known an effective solution to alcoholism and drug addiction is available, so many of those drug-induced deaths could have been avoided. What is needed is for those who know the facts to say so, and now the evidence is even better established with regards to addictions, it is tantamount to manslaughter to continue without making the admissions and changes that are necessary to right these terrible wrongs.

For centuries alcoholism and drug addiction have baffled the medical profession. Why do some men and women who consume alcohol or take drugs become addicted while the vast majority does not? Why do some people who eat food become bulimic or anorexic, and some who gamble simply cannot stop? What is *it* that causes addiction? Is the malady mental, spiritual, physical, or a combination of two, or all three? Is it hereditary? Is it linked to childhood, physical or sexual abuse, social class, poverty, riches, age, more or less intelligence? The evidence suggests addiction is like human fingerprints; each case is slightly different but there are similarities.

Millions of Miracles does not provide the answer as to what causes addiction. What it does do is show how the current drugs laws and legacy of the so-called 'War on Drugs' has exacerbated the addiction problem worldwide. This is not only because it made so-called hard drug addicts into criminals, it created the perfect conditions to encourage crime through drugs cartels and gangs, causing untold numbers of deaths.

Worse still, by supporting drug substitution treatment, and pharmaceutical firms convincing politicians this works, addicts get hooked on a different drug that exacerbates their problem, because their underlying problems were not dealt with. The knock-on effect is the chaos caused by drugs and the world's drug laws today.

There is only one way to cure addiction and that is total abstinence from all addictive substances. The fact that this treatment is available, free of charge, in 175 countries throughout the world, and yet is still not put forward by the medical profession as its number-one approved treatment, begs the question: Why not?

When you take into account that 65% of people in prisons are there because they were under the influence of alcohol or other drugs when they committed their crimes, the majority of casualties in Accident & Emergency hospital units are there because of drug or alcohol-related incidents, HIV, other sexually transmitted diseases and hepatitis C cases are higher in addicts than any other group of people, it's easy to see that the benefit to society of a proven, 100% effective treatment being promoted by governments and the medical profession would be incalculable to society and the taxpayer.

But instead, the pharmaceutical industry and governments *prevent* recovery from addiction by ***not*** endorsing important facts about it being a disease and ***not*** promoting the proven effectiveness of the programmes to treat it AA has given birth to, especially Narcotics Anonymous (NA).

So, the questions are why and why? As when you know the answers, their stances are absurd.

Millions of Miracles provides the answers and puts forward a workable solution.

As well as establishing the truth about drugs, alcohol and addiction, and exposing the wrongs caused to millions because of hypocritical drugs laws, the book explores the enormous potential if hundreds of millions more recover and highlights the positive contributions this would make to the world's economies and its people.

Chapter 1

Background Facts

Most addictive drugs are legal, and barring age limits, can be obtained in bars, shops or pharmacies by almost anyone. As only some 10% of drug users have addiction problems and the other 90% use drugs for pleasure and medicinal purposes, this seems reasonable. They come in the form of sprits, beer, wine, cider, cocktails and prescription drugs. Those who take them make a personal decision to do so, and given that mankind is blessed with free will, this is the way most people think it should be.

However, what few governments seem to grasp is that to an addict, being hooked on one drug is the same as being addicted to, or dependent on, any other. If it is not alcohol, Valium, sleeping pills, codeine, methadone or fentanyl, it could just as easily be heroin, cocaine, ecstasy, LSD, crack, cannabis, glue, speed, any hallucinogenic drug, or other opiate, benzodiazepine, antidepressant, steroids or other mood-altering drug on the market. Also, whether an addict drinks, inhales, sniffs, eats, injects or gambles is irrelevant; it is the effect on their mind and/or body that cause them to crave more and take it over and over again.

So whether the drug is legal or illegal, the harmful physical and mental effects remain the same. And the massive cost to the taxpayer in terms of healthcare, hospitalisation, crime, prison sentences, and supporting the children of families wrecked by addiction, keeps going up.

The most common addictive drugs are:

Legal
- *Alcohol.*
- *Opioids:* produce a euphoric effect due to their painkilling abilities for short-term or chronic pain.
- *Tranquillisers and depressants:* include barbiturates and benzodiazepines and are some of the most abused drugs. They have a calming, relaxing effect on the brain.
- *Stimulants:* This class increases brain activity, thereby increasing alertness and energy.
- *Methadone, Subutex, Suboxone:* heroin substitution or opiate substitution withdrawal prevention drugs.
- *Antidepressants and Baclofen* are not known to be addictive, but they have been shown to cause dependency in alcoholics and drug addicts, and with some there is a history of suicides.

Illegal
- Crack/Cocaine
- Crystal Meths
- Heroin (the only illegal opiate)
- LSD
- Marijuana
- MDMA (ecstasy/Molly)

While prescription drugs and alcohol are responsible for untold misery to addicts and families alike, the categorising of some drugs as illegal has created a huge problem in terms of criminal gangs and violent crime. Illegal drugs are big business and have made some unscrupulous people unbelievably rich. Just one look at the Mexican drug cartels tells you everything you need to know about the terrible effects of illegal drugs on society as a whole, let alone the suffering of the addicts themselves. As a case in point, in 2013, it was reported that 77,000 people had been killed in drug-linked violence in Mexico in just seven years.

Current Research Statistics

According to the **UK Government's Advisory Group on Alcohol Misuse:** 1.2 million people a year are hospitalised due to alcohol, and liver disease in the under 30s has doubled in recent years, costing the economy £21 billion.

The UK Centre for Social Justice has stated that: 1.6 million people are addicted to alcohol, 300,000 to opiates, and 1 in 7 children under the age of one lives with an active alcoholic or addict.

It also revealed that in 2014 prescriptions for antidepressant medications rose from 53.3 m to 57.1 m. Many of these were given to alcoholics and addicts, which merely exacerbated their problems.

According to the **Health and Social Care Information Centre (HSCIC)** in the UK this translates into doctors prescribing antidepressants to 1 in 10 women and 1 in 20 men.

A 2013 United Kingdom National Health Service review on illegal drug abuse revealed the annual cost to the British economy is £15.4 billion, the Institute of Alcohol Studies puts the cost of alcohol abuse at £21.8 billion – total £37.2 billion.

But *not included* in these statistics, due to the UK's hypocritical drug laws, are the unmonitored men, women and children addicted to, or dependent on, prescription drugs, such as tranquillisers, sleeping pills, methadone, opiates, Suboxone, Subutex, antidepressants and Baclofen. Drugs that pharmaceutical companies claim help treat alcoholism and addiction. When, in fact, most are equally habit-forming, cost society billions of pounds, multiply immeasurably existing drug and social problems, and actually prevent recovery by causing new dependencies. But they do make huge profits for pharmaceutical companies.

Plus, there are the costs to society of food, sex, tobacco and gambling addiction whose totals are also billions of pounds, and all too often people suffering from these addictions are treated with prescription drugs.

Putting everything together means that if the right 12-Step solution to each individual's problem was applied as the primary treatment, the annual financial savings to the economy would be much more than the £24 billion the UK government receives from alcohol, gambling, and tobacco taxes.

But because of the hypocritical way the UK Government deals with drugs and the medical profession all too often treats addiction and emotional disorders, these problems are exacerbated.

In America, where the drugs laws are not much different to the UK's, they face similar, although proportionately higher, statistics.

- **The US National Institute on Drug Abuse in 2014** said that 'Abuse of tobacco, alcohol and illicit drugs is costly to our nation, exacting more than $700 billion annually in costs related to crime, lost work productivity and health care.'

- **Department of Health and Human Services in 2013**: 22.7 million persons aged 12 or older needed treatment for an illicit drug or alcohol use problem. Of these, only 2.5 million received treatment at a specialty facility. So, 20.2 million persons who needed treatment for an illicit drug or alcohol use problem did not receive it at a specialty facility that year.

- Of the 20.2 million persons who were classified as needing substance use treatment but did not receive it, 908,000 (4.5%) reported they felt they needed treatment for their illicit drug or alcohol use problem. Of these, 316,000 (34.8%) reported they made an effort to get treatment. Based on combined 2010–2013 data, the reason for not receiving treatment was a lack of insurance coverage and inability to afford it.

- Every day, thousands of youths abuse a prescription pain reliever for the first time.

- As of 2011 more Americans die from drug overdoses than in car accidents.

- **US Government DEA** report in 2013 said, '43,982 unintentional drug overdose deaths occurred in the United States, one death every thirteen minutes. Nearly 52% of those deaths, 22,767, were attributed to prescription drugs.'

As America is still ranked in the world's top three for drug-related deaths and top forty for alcohol, you might think they would be the first to jump at the opportunity to change their drug policies. But even though there is pressure from well-informed US agencies in the field of addiction and recovery, their politicians persevere with their insane attitude. Which is extraordinary considering that 12-Step recovery programmes started there, providing them with the most irrefutable evidence of how they work.

To get some idea of the global problem of addiction, we need only look at the WHO 2008 Global Report on Alcohol Consumption, which claimed: 'There are 208 million alcoholics in the world.' In 2012 they said: 'Monitoring alcohol's role in world health and disseminating effective methods of controlling and reducing alcohol-related harm are central to the mission of the World Health Organisation.'

In 2014, the **UN** stated: 'Worldwide there are 3.3 million deaths every year resulting from harmful use of alcohol; this represents 5.9% of all deaths.'

It is estimated that 10% of the world's population (WHO) has an alcohol, drug or addiction problem. As the world population is 7.4 billion (UN) that means there are 740 million alcoholics and drug addicts.

These facts show that putting the world's drugs laws right and promoting the most effective treatment to addiction and similar diseases is in the best interest of everyone everywhere in world.

So ask yourself, would you allow a single alcoholic or drug addict to run amok and ruin your life? Well, we are allowing politicians, governments and pharmaceutical companies to precisely do that with 740,000,000!

Chapter 2

Addiction Treatment

To understand why an alcoholic or addict puts lethal poisons into their bodies when they know that doing so will eventually kill them is any layman's dilemma. It is not that an addict wants to take drugs, it is that at the time their mental craving tells them they have no choice. Also, to think drug-addicted people are weak-willed is a misconception, though an understandable one since most addicts believe that one day they will quit by the use of willpower.

Like all diseases, addiction needs treating at its root cause, therefore the approach of drug substitution can never deal with the underlying condition.

The most common treatment for addiction is through so-called harm reduction. This is a philosophy that seeks to reduce the harm caused by drug use through 'a lens of public health, using accurate, fact-based drug education, drug-related illness and injury prevention, and effective drug treatment for problematic use.' (The Drug Policy Alliance)

While this may sound like a good idea in theory to some, it does not help the addict recover from their dependency because their *underlying* problems are not addressed. Harm reduction swaps one drug for another. At best, the new addiction might keep them away from drug dealers and won't land them in jail. At worst, that addict does not stop using their drug of choice, they merely take another temporarily which is added to the cocktail they already take. Not only can this be deadly, it means the cycle of dependence and addiction is never broken.

So, if there is a proven and widely available treatment for addiction, why is it not the number one recommendation by the medical profession and governments?

When the facts are analysed, the answer is clear. It is ignorance, politics and money.

By originally brainwashing the public through ignorance, politicians and the pharmaceutical industry are now trapped in a problem of their own making. Their shoot-from-the-hip greed-inspired drug policies now make it difficult for them to make the U-turn needed and support the *free* and *permanent* solution for alcoholism and addiction which they know works and which is available from AA and other 12-Step programmes worldwide. But because governments rely on alcohol, prescription drugs, tobacco and gambling for billions of pounds in tax, they avoid putting pressure on pharmaceutical companies to change the formula.

As for the pharmaceutical firms, their modus operandi has meant their drug substitution financial bonanza has grown annually for the past seventy years into a multi-billion-pound industry, and if the status quo is maintained their coffers will continue to grow dramatically.

So why would they support change? They would have nothing to gain and everything to lose financially if governments and the medical profession start promoting a treatment that is free of charge, works and involves abstinence from _all_ addictive substances – legal or illegal – _including theirs!_

The result is there is no incentive for firms such as Reckitt Benckiser, GSK (British), Pfizer – Wyeth (US), Roche, Sandoz (Swiss), Sanofi (French), TEVA (Israeli), or any other manufacturer of such drugs, to admit that their addictive or dependency-inducing drugs or drug substitutes will ever be more than a temporary fix for alcoholism or addiction.

Or such firms as Purdue Pharma, Johnson and Johnson, Pfizer, Endo (US), Novartis, Activis (Swiss) to expose the fact that their opiate products have addiction qualities _equally strong, or more so,_ than the illegal opiate, heroin.

It needs to be remembered as well, that if a prescription drug addict or alcoholic wants to take either of these drugs he or she will do so; nothing we know of in this climate of easy accessibility will stop them. Alcohol is available on every high street to anyone of a minimum age and doctors prescribe addictive drugs all too freely to deal with grief, physical pain, panic attacks or depression.

This being the case, complete prohibition would seem to be the answer, but it categorically is not. The past hundred years' history has clearly shown that prohibition only creates black markets, enriches criminal organisations and brings bloodshed and mayhem to society, at a cost of billions of dollars to the taxpayer through the increase in the rates of drug-related crime and incarceration.

In fact, it has been shown that where drugs laws have been relaxed and a more understanding attitude towards addiction adopted (page 153 Portugal), there have been enormous improvements in drug-related problems in terms of public health and the social problems associated with addiction.

This is often made worse by the regime of 'harm reduction' when it is led by the self-interest of the pharmaceutical industry, because it means addicts are prevented from dealing with the cause of their disease and underlying reasons for using drugs. Though, when it refers to clean needle exchanges it helps lessen the rates of hepatitis C and HIV.

But the way 'harm reduction' is used means the words are deceptive, leaving the public with an even greater misunderstanding about so-called 'hard' and 'soft' drugs. The fact is class A, B and C drugs are no more, or less addictive and dangerous than alcohol or prescription narcotic drugs; it is simply a case of increasing the amount the alcoholic or addict needs for a 'fix' and frequency of use.

For an addict – who will die from his disease and create mayhem in society before he or she does – to quit, they need to stop taking all addictive substances and to eradicate the reasons why they are compelled to take drugs or abuse alcohol – i.e. they need to remove the _cause_ of their addiction.

Until these facts about addiction are made public and understood by those with influence, no successful inroads to problems associated with drugs, addiction and alcoholism will occur. *Even if the world were free of all <u>illegal</u> narcotics*, a shift to alcohol, prescription drugs, food, sex or gambling for almost everyone with an addictive disorder would take place.

So, glamorising alcohol in any way, then treating its negative consequences with addictive mood-altering prescription drugs is absurd and defies all logic.

Imagine you are a visitor from another planet and are told about our world's problems with addictive drugs, the present laws and treatment. You would know in an instant the policy makers there must be insane. Because the only treatment that has a 100% success rate when it is applied is complete abstinence, and most of the world's population do not have it recommended.

Whereas when the AA and NA 12-Step programmes are practised, they are effective. This is because their founders *understood* addiction and made sure they provide the support needed to get and remain abstinent.

With regard to recovery from addiction, there is nothing more powerful than talking to someone who has done it before you. The stories of the contributors to this book – none of whom have consumed alcohol or taken mood-altering drugs for many years – is testament to the effectiveness of this approach.

Today there are many well-meaning agencies in prisons, hospitals and society all over the world offering unsuccessful solutions to addiction. This means these institutions are plagued by the same inmates and patients over and over again who were under the influence of alcohol or drugs when they committed crimes or were admitted for addiction-related treatment. In hospitals this includes the millions who suffer from gambling, food – obesity, bulimia and anorexia – drug overdoses, sexually transmitted diseases and other addictions that have come to light in the past fifty years: plus, there are the millions who die from addiction, including many aged between seven and fifteen. Solvent sniffing addicted street children in Third World countries are testament to this appalling fact.

So the need for better informed agencies that have access to solutions locally is essential. As there is no one better to assist in formulating the best solution for recovery from dependencies and addictions than former addicts, it is essential they are involved in the process. But because of the stigma the one-hundred-year-long politically driven stance has had on drug addiction, the sad fact is the public would not respect the input of former alcoholics or junkies.

However, today there are men and women from all walks of life – *including many in the medical, political, and legal professions* – who had addiction problems and used the AA and NA programmes to recover. If the world knew this, they would surely invite some of them to be the voices to pave the best way forward, not continue with the politically or financially motivated men and women who made the decisions in the past which has led to the mess regarding drugs the world is in today.

Chapter 3

Current Drugs Policies

In the face of overwhelming evidence as to the harm current drugs policies have caused, and what is possible if the best practices are put in place, it is hard to understand why governments have not changed them. A close look reveals the reasons.

a. The wrong people – politicians, drug companies and law-makers – have been responsible for assessing the problem. *Ignorance and greed.*

b. Unless you are an addict – of whatever type of substance or mood-altering emotional abuse – it is impossible to understand the *disease* of addiction. This has meant past and present laws and policies have not reflected the reality. *Ignorance.*

c. Brewers, pharmaceutical, tobacco and gambling companies have huge monetary incentives to maintain the status quo. *Financial.*

d. Politicians will not willingly change the drug laws because they hate to admit when they are wrong. *Political, financial, and fear of losing their jobs.*

A U-turn on drug policy for most governments and politicians would be tantamount to admitting that their drugs laws and the strategies used to combat drugs over the last few decades have led to millions of needless deaths from addiction and spawned drug cartels, enhanced mafias and been behind the Mexican, Columbian and American drug gang wars. To make matters worse, their stance has not done anything to remedy the situation, in fact, it has exacerbated it. The example of how the USA's prohibition of alcohol put gangsters on America's streets should have been enough to point them towards the naivety of such a move. But it did not. Instead they introduced 'the war on drugs' to highlight the criminal activities of addicts who have no control of their addiction, therefore their actions, to justify their strategy. And the net result of that is more and more deaths and no improvement, leading to America's current opiate overdose epidemic.

Some governments now seek to distance themselves from the so-called war on drugs. Yet they have not acknowledged that this policy is still far removed from that which is needed to remedy drug problems. Unfortunately, this omission leaves exposed the lack of understanding of drugs, addiction and alcoholism, and by not acknowledging it, it will continue to have an influence on the worldwide bloodshed and mayhem caused by the war on drugs approach.

In fact, the spin behind this misnomer has made the drug problem immeasurably worse. The very name and the manner in which it has been applied exacerbated the stigma of drug addiction, thereby causing more harm than good. Because as well as helping to conceal the facts, it generates contempt for certain categories of drug addict, who, as a result, have been marginalised in society and treated as scum.

Since the USA's drugs policy was first branded the 'war on drugs' in the 1970s, their global influence has wreaked havoc on the world's drug problems. And as the word 'war' is associated with guns, this policy dovetailed into America's gangster and gang culture, making it many times easier for criminals, addicts and the mentally unstable to acquire guns, thereby aiding and abetting another of the USA's crazy policies.

The trouble with this is, as the saying goes, 'When America sneezes the world catches a cold'. In this instance it is a global epidemic that has cost millions of lives and done immense harm to societies in every country in the world. Therefore, we must make sure the USA's next sneeze best serves society, addicts, their families, saves millions of lives and billions of pounds.

As these should surely be the objectives of everyone, the only question is how to do this?

Chapter 4

Is there a Solution?

Given the complicated and delicate nature of the present situation politically, medically, financially and legally, the question is:

Can it be put right? If so, how?

Given the enormity of the world's drug and addiction problems, and the depth of public misunderstanding, a workable solution can only come from the very highest echelons of the world's medical fraternity; anything less would not topple the control politicians and Big Pharma has on the situation.

To apply a workable solution, the World Health Organisation (WHO) and United Nations Foundation on Global Health (UNFGH) need to categorically endorse the fact that *addiction is a disease* and the *only* known cure is *total, permanent abstinence*. Because, as doctors, psychotherapists and psychiatrists now know, unless addicts use a solution that treats the underlying cause of their illness, they cannot recover, but when that is treated, they do. But this fact is not new. The American Medical Association (AMA) declared that alcoholism was an illness in 1956. In 1991, the AMA further endorsed the dual classification of alcoholism by the International Classification of Diseases under both psychiatric and medical sections.

The stories that follow later in this book clearly demonstrate that the symptoms of all forms of drug addiction are identical to those of alcoholism and recovery from each is possible.

The WHO and the UNFGH need to unreservedly confirm this as quickly as possible before the situation gets even worse. They already have the resources to do this using an unbiased, ethically inspired team of medical and judicial professionals to establish the facts about alcoholism, addiction, and recovery. So all they need do is to give it the go-ahead.

That should lead to the WHO removing the ambiguity caused by two misleading reports it published in 2004 which outlined the '*burden*' alcoholism and drug addiction have on other diseases, society and the economy while omitting to say that alcoholism and drug addiction are diseases themselves!

If their conclusions are the same as those contained in this book, drug treatment centres around the world, and shared by millions of alcoholics and addicts who applied the AA and NA programmes and recovered, they would also be able to put forward a strategy which would work for other forms of addiction and a range of emotional sufferers.

Doing this may need gradual implementation, but it would immediately expose the present misunderstandings and remove much of the negative stigma currently attached to alcoholism and drug addiction. It would also clear the way for medical practitioners to recommend the most appropriate treatment for each such person they treat. The directory at the end of this book will help them decide which that is.

Most importantly, it would pave the way to make politicians change drug laws. And this should open the floodgates to recovery for millions more sufferers. Recovery that is currently unavailable to millions due to the hypocritical policies outlined above.

Only when politicians own up to their ill-conceived, almost inhumane past approach to dealing with drugs, and admit that addiction is a disease, will the tried and proven programmes of AA and NA get the support they need to stop the rot. And only when millions of addicts can be helped to abstain from *all* addictive substances, *legal* and *illegal*, will the crazy double standards that have been in place for so long begin to right themselves. And with a drop in demand, both the legal and illegal drugs trade will slow down, and sanity be given the opportunity to reign.

Only then can the cost to taxpayers around the world of billions of pounds, crime and health problems, not to mention the effects on relationships and families, begin to be put right.

But all is not gloom. There are more and more medical professionals and politicians who have witnessed at first hand, through family members, patients or friends, the recovery success of AA, NA and other 12-Step fellowships. Many doctors now acknowledge the failure of drug substitution to conquer addiction to drugs and alcohol, and are aware recovery is possible through the 12-Step process. As the following stories prove, with determination and the right support, not only are these issues possible to put right, they will happen.

US president, Abraham Lincoln – known as 'Honest Abe' – worked diligently to maintain his integrity. When referring to deception, he said, 'You can fool all the people some of the time and some of the people all the time, but you cannot fool all the people all the time.'

With millions of lives and billions of pounds already lost to the world's political and business deceptions with regard to drugs, surely the time has come to put this right?

Chapter 5

Alcoholics Anonymous & Narcotics Anonymous

In 1901 Charles Towns opened a hospital in New York City specialising in alcoholism and drug addiction. In 1908, Dr William D Silkworth, who was acknowledged as one of the foremost experts on both subjects, published a paper on the failure of the then widely used drug substitute, ant opium, to cure chronic morphine and opium addiction. In 1929 he went to work at Towns Hospital, applying his belief that addiction to alcohol is a disease, *'an obsession of the mind and allergy of the body'*, that condemns alcoholics to go mad or die. This meant that _only_ total abstinence works to treat alcoholism.

Alcoholics Anonymous (AA)

By the time of his death in 1951 it was estimated Dr Silkworth had used this hypothesis to help 40,000 alcoholics, many of whom had recovered permanently. This view was reinforced by another specialist on this subject, Dr Harry Tiebout, who had joined the hospital staff as its consulting psychiatrist.

Having discovered this then revolutionary idea on one of his frequent visits to Towns Hospital, William Wilson (Bill W), a stockbroker and former alcoholic from New York, was guided to meet Dr Robert Smith (Dr Bob), a practising alcoholic who lived in Akron, Ohio. Their meeting took place on 10th June 1935 and resulted in their being the founding fathers of AA. The first female member joined AA in 1937 and first non-Christian in 1939.

The name 'Alcoholics Anonymous' is derived from its first publication – informally called by members 'The Big Book' – originally titled *Alcoholics Anonymous: The Story of How More than One Hundred Men Have Recovered,* published in 1939.

With the help of the Oxford Group – a Christian organisation that believed man's problems stemmed from fear and selfishness – and other early members, Bill W and Dr Bob developed AA's 12-Steps of Recovery Programme; this includes spiritual and character development, both deemed necessary to achieve lasting sobriety.

AA's 12 Traditions were introduced in 1946 to help the AA fellowship stay stable and unified, and not be influenced by outside issues. The Traditions recommend that members remain anonymous in the media, help other alcoholics achieve sobriety, and avoid affiliation with other organisations. They also advise that those representing AA in public arenas such as hospitals, schools, colleges, prisons and other institutions avoid religious dogma and political controversy.

Twenty years after its birth, an AA survey revealed there were more than 150,000 members in the USA, Canada, United Kingdom, Scandinavia, South Africa, South America, Mexico and Australia.

Four years later, in October 1959, Bill W wrote an article in the AA *Grapevine* magazine (AA's monthly magazine written by members) asking if AA could transcend all those formidable barriers of race, language, religion and culture; all those kinds of pride and prejudice, cross all of the barriers that had, as never before divided and shattered the world of our time?'

By the time he died sober in January 1971, he had the answer. Ever since it has spread its wings to new outposts every year.

Membership has spread across the globe to all social backgrounds, cultures, faiths and sexual persuasions. In the fourth edition of its flagship book, *Alcoholics Anonymous* (November 2001), it states: 'Since the third edition was published in 1976, worldwide membership of AA has just about doubled, to an estimated two million or more...'

By 1976 it was conservatively estimated that more than one million alcoholics had recovered using the AA 12-Steps of Recovery Programme. Thirty years later this was well in excess of two million. By 2021, with continued growth and adding those who died sober, this figure is nearer three million.

Narcotics Anonymous (NA)

In the early 1950s, alcoholics addicted to other drugs had joined the rapidly growing AA fellowship. As they came to understand that their dual drug addiction had the same symptoms as their alcoholism, they formed NA in September 1953 and created an identical programme for addicts of every mood-altering substance. This was necessary because AA is specific to alcoholism, whereas men and women addicted to other drugs needed to belong to an organisation that catered for addiction to any addictive substance, whether legal or illegal.

The first members, most of whom were in AA, were authorised by AA to use their 12-Steps and Traditions on the condition that they did not use the AA name; hence the principles of both programmes and fellowships are virtually identical.

In 1954, the first NA publication was printed. It was called the *Little Brown Book* and contained an overview of the 12-Steps and early drafts of several pieces that would later be included in NA's other literature.

Unlike the then established AA, because of the stigma of illegality associated with drug abuse, at first NA was not recognised by society as a positive force. This resulted in the initial groups having difficulty finding places that would allow them to have meetings, so often they were held in members' homes. In fact, such was the effect of this misunderstanding members had to survey meeting places to make sure meetings would not be busted by the police!

It was many years before NA became recognised as a beneficial organisation, although some early press accounts were positive. The problems were often because NA groups veered from following the 12 Traditions guidelines for groups, which were quite new at that time, the lack of structure causing serious teething issues, to the extent that meetings declined in the late 1950s, and there was a four-month period in 1959 when there were no meetings held anywhere at all. Soon after this the original founders were spurred into action, restarting NA, and applying the Traditions.

The effect of giving it a formal structure similar to AA's has resulted in the worldwide success of NA today.

In the early 1960s, meetings began to form again and grow. The NA *White Booklet* was written in 1962 and became the heart of NA meetings and the basis for all subsequent NA literature. At that time NA was called a 'hip pocket programme' because the entire literature could fit into a person's hip pocket. This booklet was republished in 1966 as the NA *White Book* and included the personal stories of addicts similar to those contained in this book - see page 73 and onwards.

The NA telephone service started in 1960 and the first Hospitals and Institutions (H & I) sub-committee was formed in 1963. Also, that year the World Service Board was formed to ensure that NA stayed healthy and directly followed the Traditions. Growth was slow, but the fellowship was learning what was effective and what was not as relapse rates declined over time and teething problems decreased.

The 1970s was a period of rapid growth in NA's history. In 1970, there were only 20 regular weekly meetings, all of them in the United States. Within two years there were 70, including meetings in Germany, Australia and Bermuda. By 1976, there were 200 regular meetings, including 83 in California alone, and others in Brazil, Canada, Columbia, India, Ireland, Japan, New Zealand and the United Kingdom. Five years later, there were 1100 meetings all over the world. A World Service Office was officially opened in 1977. In 1971, the first NA World Conference was held, and others have followed annually. At the time of writing there are at least 63,000 meetings a week in 133 countries and it is growing.

Other 12-Step Recovery Programmes

Many more addiction recovery programmes have been born from AA's. Each has been adapted to address a specific problem from a wide range of substance and/or dependency abuse issues. These self-help organisations, often known as 'fellowships', with worldwide membership of hundreds of thousands, employ the same 12-Step principles to recover.

Demographic preferences related to the addicts' drug of choice has led to the creation of such fellowships as Cocaine Anonymous (CA), Crystal Meths Anonymous (CMA), Pills Anonymous (PA), Marijuana Anonymous (MA) and Nicotine Anonymous.

Behavioural addictions such as gambling, crime, food, sex, hoarding, debtors and work are addressed in fellowships such as Gamblers Anonymous (GA), Overeaters Anonymous (OA), Food Addicts in Recovery, Sexual Compulsives, Sex and Love Addicts Anonymous (SLAA), Sex Addicts Anonymous (SAA), Emotions Anonymous, Clutterers Anonymous, Debtors Anonymous (DA) and Workaholics Anonymous.

Auxiliary groups such as Al-anon, Alateen, Families Anonymous (FA) and Nar-Anon, for friends and family members of alcoholics and addicts, respectively, are part of a response to treating addiction as a disease that is enabled by family systems.

Co-Dependents Anonymous (CoDA) addresses compulsions related to relationships, referred to as co-dependency.

Today, through word-of-mouth, AA and NA have helped 3,500,000 alcoholics and addicts recover. This is because they provide a programme of recovery that deals with the causes.

Chapter 6

How AA and NA Work

Whether it is addiction to tranquillisers, sleeping pills, methadone, Suboxone or Subutex – all legal, addictive drug substitutes that do not work to cure addiction; or alcohol, 'legal highs', crack, heroin, cocaine, cannabis, opium, LSD and Ecstasy – which except for alcohol and 'legal highs' are illegal; or an addict dependent on antidepressants, Baclofen or Antabuse, the Alcoholics Anonymous and Narcotics Anonymous programmes work for any alcoholic or drug addict who applies them.

So why have the 12-Step programmes been so successful, when the treatment put forward by pharmaceutical companies and applied by most of the world's medical profession at best neutralises the problem, but mostly exacerbates it?

It is primarily because they provide programmes of recovery designed by alcoholics and drug addicts whose lives depended upon it. And the *only* requirement for AA or NA membership is a desire to stop drinking alcohol or taking drugs. Their primary purpose is to help their members achieve abstinence and remain that way.

The 12-Step Programmes work by dealing with the causes of addiction. The constituents are practical and serve to straighten out one or more of the kinks in an addict or alcoholic's thinking that developed during their active addiction and formative years. For example, instead of blindly repeating the same mistakes again and again, they regularly examine themselves, keep what helps them grow, and discard what does not: denial is counteracted by admission, secretiveness by openness, lying by honesty, arrogance by humility, fear by faith, isolation by fellowship, greed by charity, and self-centeredness by freely serving others.

Each of these changes is essential to achieving total and permanent abstinence. They are brought about by adapting the simple principles contained in the programmes which are specifically designed to suit those with addiction problems that are out of control and remove the layers of fear, resentment and self-hatred that accumulated during their years of alcoholism and/or other drug addiction.

The essence of the programme is for members of their chosen fellowship to share their experience, strength and hope with one another as to how they solved their common problem and make every effort to help others recover from alcoholism and/or other drug addiction.

Most importantly, each fellowship's 12 Traditions protect their members from external and internal potentially destructive influences. There are no leaders, only trusted servants; everyone is equal; the aim is to attract rather than promote. There are no dues or fees for membership; they are self-supporting by members' contributions.

And to make sure there are no outside influences, neither AA nor NA are allied with any sect, political party, religious denomination, organisation or institution; they do not engage in any controversy, neither endorse nor oppose any cause. Their members' primary purpose is to stay alcohol and drug free and help other alcoholics and drug addicts get and stay clean and sober.

Whereas AA with regard to alcoholics, and NA with regard to drug addicts the founders had only one objective when they created their abstinence-based programmes: to develop a solution that resulted in freedom from all mood-altering chemicals and lifelong recovery for any addict or alcoholic who applied them. Whereas pharmaceutical companies are motivated by money. Their persistence with drug substitutes suggests that either they do not want to lose the huge amount of revenue they earn through producing these drugs, or they still believe there may be an alternative remedy despite all the evidence to the contrary that alcoholism and addiction are diseases of the mind and body which cause those who are addicted to have an uncontrollable mental craving and/or allergic reaction.

Using the evidence now available shows this needs correcting as the vast majority of alcoholics and illegal drug addicts are still treated as social outcasts. But in many ways the situation is much worse, because, as explained above, it has meant many who suffer are given prescription drug substitutes by doctors and psychiatrists, so they have become dually addicted.

Another worrying fact is that these dependency-creating drugs upon which the addict or alcoholic is 'parked' have not been on the market long enough to know what the real long-term side effects will be. And given that the alcoholic or addict is still getting their fix from a mood-altering drug, because their underlying craving for drugs has not been removed, there will not be the necessary behaviour or spiritual changes he or she needs to make, so they will return to their former mental state or worse if ever they stop taking them.

Equally worrying is that when an addict or alcoholic is put on a drug substitute their thinking becomes foggy and their mind blocked from understanding how to work a 12-Step programme. The knock-on effect of this is that when they return to their former habit, perhaps committing crimes or suicide, the public receive entirely the wrong message as to the effectiveness of 12-Step programmes which work whenever they are applied, _and the side-effects are only ever good._

As they are free and there are only positive results, it is essential this message is made available to everyone who needs it. If pharmaceutical firms had such proven results and statistics, they would be knocking government doors down to put right the world's drug laws and have all doctors prescribe their products.

So why don't the WHO and UN recommend the most effective method known to work for all those who need treatment? There surely can be no excuse, given that AA, NA and many other 12-Step programmes are available in 175 countries in 80 languages.

Part 2

The Miracles

To illustrate the success of 12-Step programmes and how they have transformed lives, the following stories have been written by former alcoholics and addicts from a range of social backgrounds, religions, sexual orientations, professions and nationalities. In addition, the variety of substances the writers used ranges from those categorised as legal and illegal, to food, sex and other forms of emotional disorders.

Whether it was cocktails in Manhattan bars or cannabis in Amsterdam coffee shops; prescription drugs in Harley Street clinics or heroin in Hong Kong dens; opium on the streets of Iran or whisky in Saudi Arabian compounds; solvent sniffing street children in Moroccan slums or cocaine in Paris night clubs; binging on food at home, gambling in Las Vegas casinos or paying for sex in Hamburg, the results for addicts were the same. Their lives spiraled out of control, despite repeated attempts to stop their addiction.

The stories are at first harrowing, then full of hope, and finally inspiring. The honesty and courage of each individual gives reassurance to others similarly addicted that there is a way back from the hell they have descended into. They just need to find the right help. It is there for anyone, and everyone is welcome. And it is always free.

Chapter 7

Jack's Story

There once was a man who did not have the foggiest notion what he wanted to do with his life, and to make it foggier still, for twenty-five years he befuddled his mind further with copious quantities of prescribed narcotic drugs and vast amounts of alcohol. As a result, he unwittingly descended into one of the worst kinds of nightmare known to mankind: the living hell of drug addiction and chronic alcoholism. I know this is true because that man was me. My name is Jack. I am a former drug addict and an alcoholic.

Aged forty, I was one of the hundreds of thousands of people in the United Kingdom hooked on prescription drugs – sleeping pills and tranquillisers –and addicted to alcohol. Each of these drugs was legal, easily available and came with no health warnings. So, unbeknown to me when I first drank beer aged fifteen in a local bar, and took Valium aged twenty prescribed by my doctor, each was a potential killer, and when combined this possibility was much greater. In the ensuing twenty-five years I got as close to death from using this cocktail of drugs daily as is possible without dying.

In July 1985 I was confronted with the seriousness of my situation by an addiction counsellor while being assessed for admittance to Charter Clinic in Hampstead, London for alcoholism. Before that day I had no idea of the danger I was in. (I was also one of millions addicted to cigarettes, at least 30 a day, who first smoked aged 14 long before health warnings for smoking became obligatory.)

After seven weeks of total abstinence the fog of all the prescription drugs I had taken for two decades began to lift. Before then my mind was too hazy to comprehend anything except the severity of my drug abuse. In that time, I had come to understand that I suffered from the disease of drug addiction, but if I followed the set of simple principles outlined in AA and NA's recovery programmes, I need never take mood-altering substances again.

For the past thirty-five years I have precisely done that. But unlike Alice, my wonderland was an alcohol and drug-fuelled nightmare, not a dream, and to begin with I was convinced that life without drugs would be impossible and boring. Fortunately, there were new clean and sober friends who were months or years ahead of me who kept assuring me it would be the opposite.

First, I needed to erase the debris of my past which for years had hung over me like a lead weight. Fortunately for me, this is one of the respects where the AA and NA 12-Step programmes score maximum points in early recovery. In the following months I worked through their suggested 12 Steps with the help of a sponsor, a former sufferer himself. As a result I have come to live in the real world along with millions of other former alcoholics and addicts of every known addictive drug who have followed the same path and conquered their personal battle with the disease of addiction.

My recovery was a drawn-out process and is ongoing; patience, practice, and endurance have been needed, as well as courage and blind faith that things would improve when life got tough, as it often did. In that time the drug-induced veils that had clouded my mind and dogged my existence lifted. My mental faculties returned, enabling me to start a new way of life.

The overall result is that I found a purpose for my life, one I would never have dreamed possible; one that is also hugely rewarding. That purpose is to be one of the millions who pass on the NA and AA message of recovery from drug addiction and alcoholism to as many who are similarly afflicted as possible. Since that first summer, I have been able to do that, and my life has always continued to get better.

****

1st August 1985

Where in hell am I...? I am lying down and not alone. I have a blurred image of figures standing around me.

One of them, dressed in ghostly white, bends forward and says, 'You had an epileptic fit. You have been unconscious for some time.'

I don't say a word, I am instantly petrified. Is this a living nightmare? A few moments later the same person speaks again, this time louder.

'I have been giving you oxygen. I'm the doctor who admitted you three days ago. My name is Jan. You're in Charter Clinic being treated for drug addiction and alcoholism. Do you remember?'

I have only a vague recollection of what he is talking about. Then another of the blurred figures, a young woman standing next to him, who is also in white, says, 'I'm a nurse; your room-mate found you. You're fortunate. It was just in time.'

Jan puts a mask over my nose and mouth and says, 'You need more oxygen: just breathe in and out slowly. After that we can talk.'

I could not believe what was happening. I had no idea what had led up to this situation and was too dumbstruck to reply. I drift off and after a while, slowly open my eyes. I am alone with Jan, who is now sitting next to me.

After a few words of reassurance, he says, 'I used to be a doctor on Dutch ships. Just like you, I was an alcoholic, tranquilliser and sleeping pill addict, in other words a chronic drug addict. I had reached the lowest point in my life and knew that if I didn't quit, I'd end up in the morgue.'

I was mesmerised and terrified. No one had ever said such words to me before. My mind started to work and rationalise as it had every day for the past twenty years. I thought, *But my condition is not that bad? All I take are drugs prescribed by doctors and drink wine! People like me are not alcoholics or drug addicts!*

'How long have I been like this?' I feebly asked.

'I'm not sure for how long you lost consciousness,' Jan replied.

As I looked around little things started to come back to me. *But what had happened for me to be lying on this bed in this hospital ward?*

Jan must have known what I was thinking. He summed up my situation in words I will never forget.

'I read your psychiatrist's notes. The amount of Valium, Ativan, and sleeping pills you took every day for the past twenty years would have killed an elephant. I have never known anyone take what you did and drink so much alcohol at the same time, for so long. Your tolerance rose to extraordinary levels. It is similar to what mine was nine years ago.'

He paused to make sure this identification sank in; then continued.

'I started to go to Alcoholics Anonymous and worked its programme of recovery. This saved my life. I hope you will let it do the same for you. If you do not, you will end up dead, with a wet brain or in prison.'

'But I have been to AA and it didn't help,' I answered.

'Just going isn't what I said. It is working its programme of recovery that is the lifesaver.'

****

April 1984

Where in hell am I...? I cannot remember anything. I am lying on a bare stone floor and all I can see around me are men's legs and bodies! I raise my gaze a little and see bars. I gradually realise I am in a prison cell.

How long have I been here? How did I get here? are the questions that start spinning in my terrified mind.

But my hangover is no different to the thousands I have had in the past twenty-five years, but never had I found myself in such a position as this before. I continue to lie there, going through the events of the previous twenty-four hours as best I can remember them. I am in 'blackout', a condition I am awfully familiar with – unable to remember what I had done the night before.

I had started drinking at San Francisco's airport just before boarding my flight to Los Angeles. I drank more on the flight and more in Los Angeles on arrival. I had flown in from London two days before, and except for sleeping, I had been drinking and taking drugs around the clock.

I had an arrangement to stay with a woman who lived in Santa Barbara. I had assumed this was a suburb of Los Angeles and that she would meet me at the airport. Geographically speaking, I was a long way out – Santa Barbara is a good distance from Los Angeles, and she had meant she would meet me at the airport in Santa Barbara! By the time I met her I was already in bad shape.

It was early evening and she quickly appraised my condition. She said, 'You're acting very strangely. There's something seriously wrong with you.'

I knew she was right and tried to joke about it. When we had met at a Club Med in Spain a few months earlier we had established a common bond in relation to drugs, so I was quite surprised when she said, 'I am not having you to stay with me. You're far too sick and make me feel scared.'

Shortly after that she dumped me at a motel. From that moment on I can hardly remember anything, though I vaguely remember falling down some steps and into a bar, also falling into some bushes when I thought I had seen a police car.

As I lay on the floor of the jail, I realised I badly needed a tranquilliser fix. I searched my pockets and found there was nothing in them. As I always kept 30 to 50 milligrams of Valium or Ativan on me for such emergencies, I started to panic. I got to my feet, fully comprehending for the first time that I was in the biggest police cell I had ever been in and there were other men in it with me.

I went to the cell door and asked to see someone. Eventually someone came and I explained my situation that I was a British holidaymaker. None of the rest of what happened then do I remember except that there was a lot of controversy about my not having a passport or any other means of identification, coupled with talk of deportation!

It was eventually decided that I would be taken by police car in search of my motel. As we drove off, I turned around and read a huge sign, 'Santa Barbara State Penitentiary'. For the first time I knew where I was!

We drove a few miles to the area where I had been picked up the night before. After several attempts, we found the motel at which I had registered, and fortunately for me, on the bed were my passport, flight details, and ticket home. There was also my supply of Valium.

It was suggested by the officers accompanying me I leave the country as soon as possible. I did not need telling twice.

****

February 1984

Where in hell am I...? As I slowly surfaced from the deepest of comas and blackouts, all I knew was that I was in a bed and it was not my own!

As my eyes gradually adjusted to the dim light, I moved my hands and began groping around. First, I realised the bed was soaking wet; then that I was naked and someone equally naked was lying next to me, facing the other way. My first thought was, *Please* let her be attractive, not hideous, and my second, not another prostitute.

On this occasion only the second of my desires was answered!

In many ways I was used to this situation, but usually it happened at my place in central London in familiar surroundings. Anticipating a rollicking for wetting the bed, and because of the embarrassment that I was already consumed by, I moved as stealthily as I could to the edge, then started to sidle off.

As my feet touched the ground a female voice said, 'Oh, you're awake. I thought you'd died. Where do you think you are going?'

I literally froze because I recognised it from a previous encounter of the most horrendous type. In all my dallyings in drunken stupors with the opposite sex that one had been the worst. Her name was Yvonne and the same thing had happened once before at my place after I'd met her at the nightclub, Stripes, in Kensington.

But where was I this time?

I could not face turning around as I now felt sick. It was not so much that Yvonne was ugly, it was more the shame and remorse that I'd had sex with someone I found so repulsive. Somehow or other I managed to say, 'Hi, Yvonne. Another good night. I hope it was the same for you.'

'No, it wasn't. You were rude and the sex was awful. Don't ever ring me at one o'clock in the morning again feigning suicide; that's the umpteenth time you've done it and before I'd always had the sense to say no.'

I was dumbstruck as I could not believe what she had said. I knew I had a list of girls I would ring when I was feeling sexy and lonely, but was gobsmacked. She had many times turned me down! Also, I was terrified of dying… had I really been contemplating taking my own life? I eventually mumbled, 'I'm sorry, I just wanted to see you. I didn't mean it about suicide…' and my voice trailed off.

As she did not reply and I was now slightly more compos mentis, I said as casually as possible, 'Do you know where I left my clothes?'

'In the living room where you took them off. But now you're sober, why don't you come back to bed and make it up to me?'

Her words and my corresponding thoughts made me desperate for a massive tranquilliser fix. As I mentioned earlier, I always kept a supply of Valium or Ativan in the pockets of my trousers as I was terrified of running out.

'I need a cigarette. I'll be back in a minute,' I said.

As nonchalantly as I could I went out of the bedroom and into the living room. As quietly and in the shortest time possible I dressed and got out of the apartment, leaving the front door open so as not to make a noise. From the view on the outside terrace I saw I was on the fourth floor of a tower block and took the stairs, not daring to wait for the lift. When I got outside, I walked as closely as possible along the side of the building until I reached a road. Then I looked back at what I assumed was a council estate and knew I was somewhere I had never been to before.

By now I was desperate and searched through my pockets for a more-than-ever-needed Valium fix. To my horror they were almost empty: no drugs and just £2.

Before that morning I had no idea what panic attacks were, but in the course of the next few hours I found out. During those hours I was convinced I was going to die from a nervous breakdown and/or tranquilliser withdrawal.

After almost two hours wandering unknown streets that all looked the same and getting more and more lost, I asked and was told I was in Burnt Oak in North London. Not knowing where that was, and after what seemed an exceptionally long wait, I caught a bus to King's Cross. From there I took the Tube and eventually arrived home late afternoon in the most awful mental and physical quivering state I had ever known. My Marble Arch flat had never been more welcoming; but it was not its luxury I was pleased to return to but the relief of knowing that here I had tranquillisers and alcohol galore.

****

When I got sober in the summer of 1985 and looked back on the last years of my alcoholism and drug abuse, I saw that incidents like these happened regularly and blackouts daily. Sometimes I knew I was better off not remembering, but sometimes as I verged on the brink of chronic addiction, I wished I had been sober to enjoy the moment!

Late one Sunday morning I was gaining consciousness when the phone rang. It was Mark, one of the hosts from the party I had been to the night before. He and his twin brother Jeremy were friends from my tennis club, Campden Hill, and lived in the prestigious Palace Court in Kensington.

'I was wondering how you are. You were in a bad way when you left this morning.'

Perplexed and always defensive under such blacked-out circumstances, I replied, 'I'm fine, just a slight hangover. That's all.'

'Good. In that case, why don't you drop in for brunch? A few people stayed last night, and we'll be eating soon.'

After putting the phone down, I tried desperately to play back what I could remember; sadly, it was very little.

Soon after I had arrived at the party, with confidence oozing from several early-evening cocktails, I surveyed the scene. Talking casually to two men was one of the most attractive women I had ever seen. Her exquisite face, pouting lips, long black hair and a figure that her tight roll-necked black sweater and grey cross-checked mini skirt highlighted to perfection, had me spellbound.

Making sure I had a large drink in my hand, I asked Mark to introduce us. In my transfixed lustful state all I heard was, '... and Christine, this is Jack. He's a friend from the tennis club I just joined.'

My barrister hosts were wealthy and had expensive Conran furniture throughout their sumptuous apartment. In an annex I knew there was a fountain and swing sofa-seat, just right for romance. After a reasonable time, I suggested we went in there as I also guessed it would be quiet. With no hesitation she accepted, and as both our glasses were empty, I went to the bar for drinks. From then on, I did not remember anything.

By the time I was back at Palace Court the following day my hangover veils had partially lifted, and I was feeling reasonable. After what seemed like introductions to people I had never met before, I sat down. As Mark handed me a plate of smoked salmon and scrambled eggs on toast, with typical British public-school matter-of-factness he said, 'What did you think of Christine? I was surprised you did not pursue her. She seemed interested. Maybe her reputation frightened you off.'

I was confused, but my dishonest mind came up with what I thought was a good answer. 'Not my type.'

'I'm impressed. Not many guys would turn down Christine Keeler,' he replied.

Oh my God, neither would I if I'd known, raced across my mind, but I was too numb to reply. I literally stared at the plate and suspect my face turned the colour of the eggs.

For years I regretted my drunken stupor that night and to this day do not know what happened. But at the time I was too ashamed to tell Mark that I had been in blackout. I knew that disclosure would expose my now rampant alcoholism.

By then that was how it was with every similar occurrence when challenged by friends or family. Although such experiences were no longer surprises, each I always defended with lies.

When I added this to my other immoral behaviour, it meant I had reached a point of total despair and utter self-loathing as to whom I had become. Inwardly, I knew alcohol and drugs were my problem, but they had imprisoned me and there was no way out, and all the time it was getting worse.

On reflection, I was baffled in my early years of recovery as to why I did not try to stop sooner. Had I lost my sanity? Later I realised it was the stigma of knowing I was a dipsomaniac and pill-head junkie that had made it so hard to admit it. Sadly, there are still millions trapped because they are tarred with the same brush. And that is because society has not been made aware by the medical profession that alcoholism and drug addiction are diseases.

****

Lack of artistic, intellectual and sporting accreditations had caused me to be rebellious and dishonest in my adolescence. Adding these to the horrendous knock-on effects of my daily intake of alcohol and prescription drugs over twenty-five years meant at age forty my self-esteem had sunk to zero. By then, as far as I was concerned, I was a blight on society and the world would be far better off without me.

Complete weeks were blacked out. I frequently wet the bed, had morning shakes, arrests for drunkenness in the USA, France and the UK, numerous alcohol-related hospitalisations – including one on honeymoon in Jamaica! Twice I lost my driving license, caused car accidents, was sacked, had sex with prostitutes and caught sexually transmitted diseases; lost most of my friends, was regularly drunk on Antabuse – which on each occasion I knew could have killed me – was too ashamed to see my family and only left my apartment when I was so drugged-up or had drunk enough not to care. My bed reeked of urine and the state of my flat was a pit. In other words, I hated everything about myself and my life.

Unbelievably, during this time, I often thought, one day if it gets too much I will stop. But deep down inside I knew I was beaten, and that thought did not last long.

To hammer my predicament home, I often recalled how two working-class men I grew up with, Eric and Trevor, had died the most horrible, prolonged deaths from alcoholism caused by drinking 'scrumpy' – cheap, rough, bitter cider. I knew I was heading in the same direction on a vastly more socially acceptable cocktail, but the result would be identical.

A life spent living in hell on earth was **not** something I'd aspired to in my teens; I'd wanted to be a stockbroker, journalist or barrister, not an out-of-work alcoholic and drug addict. Yet the path I was following was Eric and Trevor's. No wonder in AA and NA they call addiction 'the disease of insanity'.

What causes a once innocent person to fall into such a hopeless bottomless pit? and What, is the way out? are the questions the rest of this book endeavours to answer.

Chapter 8

Me, an Alcoholic & Drug Addict!

I had grown up in an honest, loving family in the beautiful Wye valley in Wales; so how had I become a self-obsessed, dishonest, terrified, lonely, unemployable individual? What happened to cause this and why had life crashed around me?

I reflected on my childhood. I wondered, for example, where I had got my rebellious and dishonest streaks from. My parents were not like that and had taught me a high moral code. The trouble was I broke almost every principle my parents and teachers taught me in my formative years, so, from an early age the ways I lied and stole led me to believe I was a fundamentally awful person. And because my bad habits got worse during the next twenty-five years, my self-loathing grew exponentially. I was told alcoholism is often hereditary, but there was no one in my large family who had a drink or drug problem.

As I looked back further, I recalled how I had always been in trouble in school, thrown out of both the Cubs and Boy Scouts. That sort of thing does not happen to 'nice little boys', so why, my conscience asked, had it happened to me?

Am I all bad, insane, or even evil? And where do my many fears come from?

For as long as I could remember I had shoplifted, been afraid of pain and death, lied and cheated and had an ego the size of which would have daunted Freud! (And when it was discovered aged fifteen one of my testicles had not dropped, I was christened in school 'Alf-the-one-balled-wonder', smashing my ego into tens of thousands more pieces.)

A snake sliding across my leg on a mountain when I slept, aged ten, and my sister waking me screaming that I was about to be bitten to death, left me with a phobia of dying which I blew out of all proportion.

So, was it anything to do with either of these, I wondered.

My work and sex life had both been disasters.

Maybe they were the causes?

I had numerous jobs ranging from policeman to ticket tout, salesman to sales manager to training consultant. I had worked for major multinational companies and run my own business consultancy. In between I had done insider dealing on the stock market, run my own property-letting portfolio, been sacked for fiddling expenses, put a company into receivership and twice been on the dole: mostly in that order.

With regard to sexual relationships I had been slow off the mark. My 'Alf-the-one-balled-wonder' label inhibited me from having sex until I was twenty-three. After that alcohol and Valium gave me confidence and I made up for lost time. My girlfriends ranged from nice working-class girls to English public-school roses, sexy French women to a rich, married German, and eventually to prostitutes.

By the time I went into my fifth addiction treatment centre I still could not see that all my troubles were because of my alcohol and drug intake. It was bad enough having been cast aside by my friends and blaming them for deserting me, but worst of all, my many shortcomings meant, aged thirty-nine, I loathed myself.

As soon as I woke up every morning my first action was to put my hand under my bed seeking the prescribed tranquillisers I had put there the night before. This I did every day as I knew I would need them to help me over the deepening depression I always felt upon wakening. Plus, each day this feeling was exacerbated by a hangover and fear of what I might have done in blackout. Once I had 'fixed' myself with Valium or Ativan and taken liquid to deal with my dehydration, I was more or less ready to face the ominous day which I knew lay ahead.

But thanks to Dr Jan's bedside chat at Charter Clinic, Primrose Hill, on the 1st August 1985, and the support of hundreds of members of AA and NA in the following months, something changed and the 'Humpty Dumpty' in me that had a great fall began to be put back together to live a life beyond my wildest of dreams.

Chapter 9

Jack's Recovery

My recovery began when I first accepted that I was an alcoholic and a drug addict. This was soon after Dr Jan spoke to me in the hospital. I knew from then on I had only one place left to turn, Alcoholics Anonymous.

The terror of not doing this meant that as I had reached the point when I would have had both my arms and legs amputated to buy my freedom from booze and drugs, AA was a better option. The solution Jan had described was simple: it was free, available all over the UK, anyone who has a drink problem could join, and it works for everyone who applies it.

For me, this unintentional and uninvited experience happened out of the blue, but as the saying goes, 'When the pupil is ready, the teacher appears!' I was ready and the teacher had appeared. But Jan was not the first.

It was the end of summer in 1984 when my 'fairy godmother' first appeared in the ultimate of disguises in Draycott's singles wine bar in Knightsbridge. I was drunk. I had been drinking all day at a Lord's cricket match. She came and stood next to me, immaculately dressed, extremely attractive, sober, and I soon found out she was quite well off. I, on the other hand, was out of work and three-quarters of the way to another night of alcohol-fuelled oblivion.

In the true love story that follows, within a few months she wanted to marry me and raise a family! I could hardly believe it. Where had this angel come from? How could this happen when she knew I was a dipsomaniac? However, she did not know I also had a chronic drug problem.

I did not argue with her marriage wishes and neither did Paddy O'C, my psychiatrist, when I told him; though even he could not have known the effect meeting her was going to have on the rest of my life.

Although it seemed sheer madness at the time, even to me in my very hazy state, it turned out that getting married at thirty-nine was the best thing I had ever done. Not only did a contact through our marriage lead to saving me from my addictions, I now had someone who could tell me daily what I had done the night before: an illumination that had been sadly lacking for lots of years.

Unfortunately, though, due to the massive quantities of prescription drugs and alcohol I had consumed each day, also for many years, there was a trail of debris to clear up and our relationship quickly hit rocky ground. For example, due to my below par moral standards, I already had a part-time live-in girlfriend in one of my London flats, and another whom I had asked to marry me who lived in Houston, Texas. Both needed sorting out before I could move on to marrying my dream woman.

When I quit all mood-altering drugs a few months later, a new light shone on my cumulative activities over the preceding months as well. For example, my lovely wife, a St. John's Wood Jewish 'princess', was able to remind me of a skiing holiday we went on with some of our friends in Switzerland earlier that year. I had no recollection of it whatsoever. I did not know where we had stayed, with whom we had been or that we had even gone – to begin with I did not even believe it had happened! As time went by, I remembered the tiniest bits of it, but that was all, and that is the way it has always been.

She also reminded me that our marriage had not started off too well. She told me how I had been hospitalised for smoking ganja and eating magic mushrooms on our honeymoon in Jamaica.

My father-in-law, a most generous businessman, had provided us with a two-and-a-half-week honeymoon on this lovely island. I was almost broke, and he paid for everything, as he had done from the moment I met his daughter. Firstly, we stayed with friends of mine just outside Kingston before moving on to the luxurious Jamaica Inn. After a few days there, we went to the far end of the island to stay at Hedonism II, a resort notorious for living up to its name.

This was my kind of place, since smoking ganja was the in thing. I hooked up with some doctors from New York who were going to a magic mushroom and ganja cake-eating party. These were my kind of people. My wife was happy to come along, too, as I was not drinking, only taking drugs, and they were an amusing crowd. All went well for the first few hours. The problem was, once I started using drugs I could never stop. I eventually ended up with horrendous hallucinations, thinking I was going insane or about to die, and being taken to hospital. There I was pumped full of Valium and gradually calmed down. Now I knew what my wife meant about our marriage not starting off too well.

As I said, though, getting married was the best thing I have ever done. This was so in more ways than just improving my memory. For weeks, my wife had been telling me how her best friend had been off alcohol for several years. She suggested I meet up with her. I did so one Saturday afternoon at her Notting Hill home. I was fully 'loaded' and not in the mood to stop drinking. She suggested we meet again the following week and that she would take me to an Alcoholics Anonymous meeting where she would introduce me to some friends who had also quit. This we did, and there I met people who were just like me; people who had been hooked on alcohol and many on other drugs too. The difference was that they were all drug and alcohol free! I could not believe it; for years I had thought there was no one else like me on the planet.

It was suggested we meet again and go to another meeting, and we did a few days later. This time I was introduced to an Australian woman who had been clean and sober – off drugs and alcohol – for a long time. She told me about a friend of hers who was the doctor specialising in alcoholism and drug addiction at the Charter Clinic in Hampstead, North London. She gave me his telephone number and suggested I ring him. That evening I did, and he thought I should meet a counsellor there called Bobby, to be assessed.

Next day I made an appointment to meet Bobby and saw her a few days after that. I turned up alcohol-free but full of tranquillisers. The great things about 'tranx' are that, as well as being legal, they do not smell and have no obvious visible side effects, so no one could ever tell when I had taken them, or how many. We talked for a long time, and although I was truthful about my alcohol intake and its consequences, I did not mention the prescribed drugs.

For several years, on and off, I had often not drunk on Sundays. Instead I would fill myself full of tranquillisers all day and sleeping pills when I went to bed at night. I kidded myself that I could not be an alcoholic if I did not drink every day of the week, fifty-two weeks of the year.

As well as fooling myself, I *almost* fooled Bobby!

We had spent an hour discussing my arrests, blackouts, bed-wetting, shakes, diarrhoea, hospitalisations and other delights surrounding the less attractive aspects of my drinking. But then she shrugged and said, 'Your drinking is certainly different. I have never met anyone who drinks as much and as often as you do but who can stop just like that.' And with that she started concluding our meeting.

I stood up to leave and started to walk towards the door. Suddenly, as if inspired, I turned and made the most world-changing statement that has ever passed my lips: Politely, I said, 'Thank you again for your time. It is easy, I just take more tranquillisers and sleeping-pills to see me through!'

I will never forget the show-stopping, earth-shattering impact of her next statement: 'Hold it right there! What do you mean, tranquillisers and sleeping pills?' she said as if she had found the answer to all the world's problems. In this case she had certainly uncovered the answer to mine.

Bobby was well made, with a dynamic, forceful, well-meaning character, and as I looked back at her beaming face, I knew it was all over for me. I was found out at last! I sat down again and this time I told her the whole story.

I had never told anyone any of the true reality of my life before, and not even my wife knew about the tranx. I was so ashamed of them. I had always thought it was only dear old ladies who took such things, not 'men': except, of course, pathetic ones like me.

As a result of my once-in-a-lifetime's honesty, I was admitted for detoxification to the Charter Clinic on Monday 29th July 1985. I have not drunk alcohol since. Two weeks later, a nurse administered my last ever mood-altering addictive pill: two milligrams of Valium. I have not taken a drug on any occasion in the intervening years and my life has changed dramatically.

I no longer spend my days in fear of dying or of meeting friends with whom I have done something shameful. I am a respected, reasonably accomplished average citizen of the world, though I hope I will never forget I am an ex-drunk and prescription pill junkie too. I have been given a role to play within my family, the work environment and in society. I run my own business and write books, which gives me great pleasure and satisfaction. I am extremely grateful to be alive and I take life as it is dealt out to me, with all its ups and downs. I have friends, both old and many new. Most importantly, I have learned how to be a friend, and to love myself.

With hindsight, I can see how the knock-on effect of meeting each of these good people, especially my wife, wondrously changed my life, and in the years that followed my perception of what life is really all about.

As a result, I have discovered the true meaning of *love*, which I now appreciate more than any of the material gifts I have been given. I came to realise in my early years of sobriety that in my drinking, drugging years I had turned all my values upside-down and back to front. I have since come to believe that there is a loving God presiding over all that there is on earth and in the universe. And I discovered that God had always been looking after me, and that this 'Higher Power' always will. As I mentioned earlier, my 'HP' has also come in many guises.

During my early years of abstinence from alcohol and prescription drugs I took up interests that I had long ago given up, but which I had loved in my childhood. I became interested again in the world of nature and the creation of our universe. In my spare time I studied astronomy, geography, geology, natural history, science, environmental issues, philosophy and the world's religions. I found a depth and meaning to life that I had not known existed, and most surprisingly of all, I learned to pray and meditate.

I changed my singular reading habits from fiction's best-known thriller writers to include the spiritual writings of Emmett Fox, Joel Goldsmith, Deepak Chopra, Wayne Dyer, Marianne Williamson, *God Calling* and *God at Eventide* by The Two Listeners, Bill Wilson, Jackie Pullinger, Thich Nacht Hanh, Mother Theresa, Mahatma Gandhi and many other spiritual or philosophically inclined authors.

I took a 'Course in Miracles' and exchanged singles wine bars, pubs and nightclubs for Alcoholics Anonymous and Narcotics Anonymous meetings, which are the most sociable gatherings I know. I visited mosques, churches, temples, synagogues and Friends Meeting Houses; the latter because I became a Quaker.

My heroes became Mahatma Gandhi, The Dalai Lama, Nelson Mandela, Mother Theresa and Martin Luther King, replacing Humphrey Bogart, Richard Burton, Dylan Thomas, Barry John, Adam Faith and Philip Marlowe – though I won't give up Raymond Chandler, watching *Casablanca*, the Barbarians beating the All Blacks in the '70s, or Wales beating England in 1999 and 2013!

I got a job I liked and was good at and went on holidays to places of interest instead of lazing at the tennis club, in bars and on beaches. To keep my mind in good shape I followed the minimum of news and listened mostly to classical music, though I did not give up Bob Dylan, Chuck Berry and the Beatles altogether.

Fear, sloth, ignorance and resentment I exchanged with courage, work, service, wisdom, and love. I give money to charities instead of pouring it down my throat, turning it into smoke, or losing it in casinos.

I discovered how to live in 'the spirit of the universe' and found that life had meaning. But most all I found freedom to be myself, though there have been some self-created potholes along the way.

But before all this I had to be detoxified. This needed close medical supervision and I was kept in the Charter Clinic detox unit for fifteen days. During this time other patients came and went, mostly staying about five nights – average for normal alcohol or drug withdrawal.

Alcohol was removed from me immediately and I quit cigarettes the same day too. A short, sharp tapering-off strategy was applied to the sleeping pills, and a more gradual one to the tranquillisers. Most of this time I was terrified. I thought they were doing it all much too quickly.

For the first three nights I hardly slept. The first night when I got out of bed to go to the loo my legs were like jelly and I literally wobbled to the floor. I had never known an experience like it and thought it was going to be like this for the rest of life. As it transpired, each night got a little bit better.

On its own I knew alcohol withdrawal could be dangerous; done at the same time as coming off tranquillisers it was horrendous. But Dr Jan, Bobby and her team of councilors convinced me I could do it and life would get better.

I was put on anti-fit pills, Epanutin, to counteract the most dangerous side-effects – epileptic fits. But due to the quantities I was coming off, and because my body had developed tolerance to them, Epanutin did not stop me having a convulsion. Fortunately, another patient was with me when it happened, who immediately called the medical staff and I was put on an oxygen machine until I regained consciousness. I knew nothing about it, which added to my fears when it was explained I might have others. Thankfully, I did not, and after a few days I was told the danger period had passed. But by then I had started hyperventilating.

When I had first been a patient at Regent's Park Nursing Home in 1980, Max Glatt, the UK's leading psychiatrist specialising in alcoholism, had warned me that sudden alcohol withdrawal was dangerous. He had prescribed Epanutin to prevent me having fits. As by now I was trying to stop drinking, frequently using Antabuse, and always failing, my fear of having such a fit helped me persuade my doctor and my other psychiatrist to add Epanutin to my list of prescribed drugs. So, by the time I got to Charter Clinic I was immune to the effect of anti-fit pills, hence my unexpected spasm whilst detoxing.

There is no doubt that my chronic fear of dying now saved my life.

While I was at Charter, I met several people who suggested I make changes to my way of life that would help me stay drug free when I left, especially Dr Jan, who whenever we met shared some of his personal experiences. I always thought it incredible that a doctor had once been like me, and that today, in his words, he was 'clean and sober'. These were the first signs of hope I had known for years. After I left, we became good friends and I will always have deep gratitude for what his little talks did for me in those early days.

The other medical staff were also kind and I soon fell in love with the female nurses – the males were good, too, but did not have quite the same soft, feminine touch! In many ways I felt as though I was carefully loved back to life. Consequently, I will never forget what they did for me. I also had regular visits from both my psychiatrists, who, once they knew the truth, found the amounts of drugs I had consumed so interesting they thought of writing it up as a case study.

In all the seven and a half weeks I stayed at Charter, about twenty patients came and went – two of them taking their own lives within a week of leaving. This did not do a great deal for my shredded confidence, but it did provide me with enough fear to make me determined to do my best to make sure their fate would not befall me. However, for the next four weeks I was convinced I was the next in line! Especially as Bobby kept reminding us in our therapy sessions that in her group of nine, she was the only one alive; all the others had died from drug-related reasons or alcoholism. Knowing my history of falling at every hurdle, it was no wonder I was worried!

About eight of us had group therapy every day where we were asked to talk about our experiences relating to alcohol and drugs; we were also urged to express our 'feelings' about anything current that caused us anxiety or resentment. It took me some time to catch on as to what was meant by 'feelings', but once I got the hang of it, I never looked back, and a lot of anger about my being an alcoholic and drug addict gradually came out. On one occasion it poured out in such abundance that I started smashing up furniture in the middle of a group session. As a result, and much to my surprise, I was taken on one side by a counsellor afterwards and told I was doing well!

Similar expressions of honesty I later found out turned the key that opened the door of my path to recovery, but after six weeks of honestly sharing like this in these group sessions, it seemed to me as if I had been 'Humpty Dumptied' and shattered into a million pieces. What worried me then was, would the counsellors be able to put me back together again? They said without hesitation they would, but it took a long time before I was convinced.

Gradually, my attitude and outlook to life changed. Alcoholics and addicts who had attended the clinic in previous years visited us and shared their abstemious living experiences. This gave me hope, something I had lacked for years. Each one told their alcohol or drug-taking story and I identified to some extent with each of them, whatever they had taken and done, however old they were, and whatever sex.

I later discovered that one of the key ingredients to recovery is for one alcoholic or drug addict to share their experience with another. I also found out that the one who reaches out to help benefits at least as much as the receiver. This is especially so when the worst things in life happen and helping a newcomer at such times will guarantee insurance against taking alcohol or drugs.

One afternoon after group the pronouncement I feared most was made: I was told I was ready to leave. Although riddled with fear, I knew at a superficial level that if ever I got into difficulties, I now had the telephone numbers of AA and NA members who would help me any time of the day or night. I was also told to get a sponsor immediately, a man who had been there, too, and was now recovered. He would act as my guide through the 12-Steps of recovery and into the corridors of living a normal alcohol- and drug-free life.

That formula worked and it still does today.

Chapter 10

Jack in Wonderland

When I had been free of alcohol and drugs for nearly two weeks, I heard something at an AA meeting that changed my life. I was still in Charter Clinic and doing all I could to remain abstinent. An older man – who turned out later to be my sponsor's sponsor – whom I knew had many years of sobriety, said, 'Every morning I get on my knees and pray to God for a clean and sober day.'

I thought, that one's wacko: I don't believe it and I've never believed in God!

Then he added, as if he had been listening to my thoughts and had said it a thousand times before, 'If there are any sceptics here tonight, when I first heard this, I was desperate enough to try anything and told to fake it to make it.' After a slight pause he added, 'At the end of the day I get on my knees and say, thank you, God, for keeping me clean and sober today.'

It was then he played his ace of trumps. 'It is *God, as you understand Him;* even a light bulb if you want it to be. And for any newcomers, I suggest you use the expression 'Higher Power', it will be easier to get your head around the concept.'

He was right. Being desperate, even I had no problem with that.

After an even longer pause, with the patience a loving father would have for a long-lost son, he said, 'In my experience, living in the day is the easiest way to view life without alcohol. More than that is too much for alcoholics like me.' Then to make it even easier, he suggested we get used to living life 'Just for Today' and 'One Day at a Time'.

I have tried to do this ever since, though not always quite as efficiently as I would have liked.

A few days later, I was having trouble with the concept of asking God to keep me sober and thanking Him at night. This time I met a long-time sober American, who suggested I think of God as though I were asking my real-life father for something, and once he had given me the 'gift', in this case sobriety, I was politely to say 'thank you'. Put like this I soon found praying easier to understand and God's 'gift' of a single clean and sober day a perfect formula to live by.

I had now finished being detoxified and was sharing a room with a cocaine addict. I had been totally drug-free for just over a week and suddenly realised this was the first time I had been without a mood-altering substance in my body for a single day in over twenty years! When I looked at it like this, I could see how diabolical my situation had become and how it was not surprising my life had got into such a mess. As I was still absolutely petrified of drinking alcohol, that night for the first time in my life, I got on my knees and prayed from the bottom of my heart.

I said something like, 'Please, God, if You exist, I beg You to help me with my drug and alcohol problems. I have tried for years to stop and failed every time. I am also terrified of dying. I promise from now on I will try to be good and lead the life I believe You would want me to.' I then added, 'Thank You, God, for the clean and sober day I've just had. Amen.'

That was it, and though nothing seemed to happen, there were no flashing lights or choirs of angels, somehow I felt good about what I had done. And most importantly of all, I was alcohol and drug free!

Next morning I was on my knees again, this time asking for help with my alcohol and drug problems for the next 24 hours, and as this action has worked for 13,085 days since, I now see that with the help of these simple prayers, which take only a few moments each day, I am sure to stay alcohol and drug-free for that day. As I have been doing this for nearly thirty-six years, I doubt I will break the routine, especially knowing it is a habit that has better results than any of the bad habits I used to have.

When I first left Charter, I was advised that staying in contact with former addicts or alcoholics would benefit my recovery. I began by ringing two daily and going to AA and NA meetings as often as I could. I found that talking to men and women who had been through the same wringer as I had, and who now lived normal drug- and alcohol-free lives, was amazingly beneficial. They introduced me to literature written by AA's founder, Bill W, and drug addicts who had recovered, and I began to read some of this daily. I found that all the structure was already in place for me to follow; tried and tested guidelines that would enable me to live a clean and sober life. All I had to do was follow the well-signposted directions. I did just that, I did not dare do otherwise. I clung to this new way of living as only the dying do. Because of fear and lingering rebellion, I found some changes hard, but with my life at stake I had become willing to do anything to stay clean and sober.

Several weeks later, shortly after returning to my wife and home in St John's Wood, I started wondering more about whether there really was a God, and if so, how did one go about finding him?

I decided to try my local Church of England on Hamilton Terrace. There, on my third or fourth visit, I sat behind two older ladies who, from the clothes they were wearing, belonged to the Salvation Army, or a similar organisation.

Just before the service started, I leant forward and asked them, 'I wonder if you can help me? How do I pray to God when I have little or no faith?'

I will never forget the reply given by the one directly in front of me. She turned around slowly, and looking over her right shoulder with the kindliest, 'I quite understand' smiles, she quietly said with the Scottish brogue of Janet from *Dr Finlay's Casebook*, 'Well, what I say every morning is, "God, I believe. Help Thou mine unbelief. Please, God, reveal Yourself to me and be real for me today."'

With that, she looked at her companion, smiled broadly as though her mission was accomplished, and returned to silently and serenely facing the front of the church.

It was so simple I was quite taken aback. Yet I knew instinctively this was the answer and desperately sought to memorise what she had said. Then, once I had it firmly etched in my mind, I leaned forward and thanked them for the treasure they had let fall into my life.

From that day forth I added these simple prayers to my 'clean and sober' request every morning. As time went by, at appropriate intervals, I was introduced to other prayers, each of which was perfect for the experience I was then going through. It was always as if my journey had been carefully mapped out and all I had to do was follow the compass signs. Since then I don't believe I have taken a single backward step, though many times it seemed I had gone forward only to encounter a huge slap in the face and end up going several back, so deeply rooted were the negative attitudes that haunted my stumbling progress. But a view of the 'big picture' clearly showed that God had always been there leading me along an ever-broadening spiritual path. And that also applied to the time when I had been incarcerated at the bottom of life's pit floundering in my self-constructed mire.

I now learned that a better sense of self-worth had to be earned in the same way that a spiritual life had to be practised. And that there were no days off in my recovery from addiction.

I found when I took positive action based on my moral beliefs, I received esteem-building results. So, on a scale of nought to ten my self-worth has risen from zero to around eight, or even nine on a good day. Conversely, when I take negative actions, I end up thinking badly about myself and slide back down the scale again to four or five. In the same way I discovered the more I practised prayer, meditation and doing charitable things for others, the more my spiritual life grew and the less self-centered I became. This often meant my having to do things I did not want to do and not doing things I would like to have done, with the net result I had a much more positive view upon life.

By my making good progress after completing much of the 12-Step recovery programme of AA and NA, my wife became keen to have a family. On several visits to my doctor I was found to have a zero sperm count, a side-effect of my alcohol and drug abuse. So there was great surprise and much delight when she became pregnant. We decided to move to a five-bedroomed house in Hampstead, have a nanny and expand our family at a later date. Someone had told me that sobriety was *'a bridge to normal living'*. I certainly had not expected anything quite like this, though I was all for it.

By now I was working as a stockbroker, which in itself had come about in a somewhat spiritually synchronistic way.

Because of my alcoholism I had not worked for several years, living on my £44,000 of savings from dubious share and property deals, plus social security. After six months sobriety and much-needed rehabilitation, both mental and physical, I had got a part-time voluntary job at London Zoo. Shortly after this I was offered full-time employment by a man in the carpet business.

He said at the interview, 'As well as everything else, you may have to clean the lavatories.'

I was horrified, but my sponsor reiterated my need for '*any* job you can get', so I took it. I had always hated getting my hands dirty and this was complete anathema to me. As it turned out, and much to my relief, I was never asked to scrub the dastardly loos. But I know I would have done it if I had been. My sponsor's words, 'You need to be willing to go to any lengths, Jack, if you intend to stay sober,' reverberated through my brain: fortunately for me, I was.

After six months full-time employment I was told by AA old-timers that I should be capable of doing something more suited to my skills. I wondered what on earth they were referring to!

Around this time, my father-in-law, a successful entrepreneur, asked me what work I would like to do for the rest of my life, or would I like to work for him? He had commercial property interests as well as wool and cashmere retail and manufacturing businesses. To the latter offer I quickly said no.

I had always wanted to be a stockbroker, but as I only had four 'O' levels and no public-school background or university degree, I had always ruled that line of work out. These aspirations had come into being after a mathematics lesson when I was about fourteen years old, when our teacher described stockbrokers and jobbers in a way that fascinated me. He also said they earned a lot of money for doing very little work, which fascinated me even more! His description had stuck with me all these years and as a result of my City contacts and nearly twenty years of dubious share dealings, I said quite abruptly and much to my amazement, 'I have only ever wanted to be a stockbroker.'

For the first time in my life I was being honest about my working ambitions. He immediately said he could fix it as his partner's son was head of Hambro's merchant bank, and 'Jimmy' Goldsmith's Number One takeover adviser. I instantly replied that I wanted to do it by myself, not for once imagining that I could actually make it happen. As it is, I do not believe I did, but that divine guidance took a hand in what happened next!

At a drinks party exactly a week later I met an older man who was quite drunk. He was friendly and after a while we got onto the subject of work. He said he was a stockbroker, and we discussed the stock market and my experiences with takeovers for quite a few minutes.

Then he asked, 'What do you do for a living?'

'I work for a carpet fitter,' I replied, then, as it was at the height of the City's 'yuppy' boom, out of the blue I added, 'However, I'm thinking of becoming a stockbroker.'

I will never forget his answer or my surprise at my directness.

'Call my office on Monday morning and I will arrange for you to have an interview. We are looking for people like you right now,' he said with an assured authority.

We spoke quite a lot more with him telling me that his firm was called Fox Milton and that they were based near St Paul's underground station. As he was getting more and more tipsy, the rest, partly due to his incoherence and my head being in the clouds, I do not recall.

I could not believe my luck, but at 9.15 Monday morning I was on the phone to his office.

It was mid-1986, the booming, pre-crash yuppie market, and at an interview the following day I was immediately offered a full-time position as a private client stockbroker. I resigned from my carpet-laying job and started a few days later. Unfortunately, I realised almost instantly that they ran a highly dodgy business.

They would buy blocks of what were tagged as 'penny shares', telephone their private clients and tell them to buy, suggesting that a takeover was imminent when it was not. The stock would be bought at say twenty pence and sold on to their clients at a slightly higher price, with commission added on top. It was scandalous and I knew I had to get out of there as quickly as possible. By now my moral values had returned and I was trying to live up to them.

As I was still very unsure of myself, I telephoned a stockbroker friend in New York who was in AA and told him what had happened. He had been sympathetic to my drink problem, and when he had lived in London a few months earlier had helped direct me towards Charter Clinic. Now, though, he was a senior executive in one of America's biggest stockbroking firms.

He said, 'You have to leave there immediately. Call the managing director of our London office and go and talk to him. I will have a word with him too.'

I did so and did not go back to Fox Milton. I had already taken my things with me the night before, anticipating something like this. It was now Friday, and three days later I was in my friend's London MD's office telling him my story. Our meeting turned into an interview and I was offered a job on the spot. I have never looked back workwise, doing something I have enjoyed ever since.

Less than a week later I was working at Jeffrey's International, Finsbury Circus, London EC2 – in The City at last! The day started for me at 7.30 a.m. Every morning I would walk across Hampstead Heath to the underground station almost skipping, I was so happy. I had always dreamed of carrying the FT and brolly in one hand, briefcase in the other and catching the Tube in the rush hour, morning and night. As far as I was concerned, I was at last doing the work for which I had always been destined.

Now for the divine guidance bit I mentioned earlier. A little over a year previously, when I had been newly dried-out, a long-time sober friend had suggested I write on a piece of paper two things I would like to have happen in the next twelve months. Then he said I should put it aside and look at it in a year's time. I wrote down:

1. Work at London Zoo

2. Become a stockbroker

I could not believe it when I remembered this piece of paper and realised what had happened. I have marvelled at the workings of Providence and my good fortune ever since.

One of my sponsor's best suggestions was that I write a **gratitude list.**

'Starting with your sobriety, write down the things you have today for which you are grateful,' he said. 'It will help you feel good about life and yourself,' he continued. 'This has been my experience and grateful alcoholics and addicts don't drink or take drugs.'

That night I wrote my first ever 'gratitude' or 'blessings' list, and he was right, it did help. Instead of my former 'Is life worth it?' thoughts, they became, 'I'm grateful-to-be-alive'. This has become a daily habit and now I keep an ongoing list on my laptop. Still Number 1 is the number of days and years I am drug and alcohol-free, because I know without sobriety, I would not have anything to be grateful for at all.

My sobriety is closely followed by my relationship with my son and the rest of my family, my spiritual beliefs, many friends, work as a mergers and acquisitions consultant and author; the travels I have made to over forty countries in my drug-free years, including trekking through the Amazon rainforest, flying up glaciers and sailing through icebergs in Greenland; piloting a helicopter and flying in a microlite in the Cotswolds; ski and summer holidays in Europe, Africa, India, China and the USA; coral reef snorkelling in the Red Sea, Caribbean and Indian Ocean. I have also been fortunate to live in my favorite parts of London, the English and Welsh countryside, and Morocco, and toured Europe alone in a motorhome for two years.

My health and the physical and intellectual gifts with which I have been blessed are also high on my gratitude list, as are the benefits I have received from practising prayer and meditation, and successfully helping others similarly afflicted with drug addiction or alcoholism.

Studying world religions, philosophy, geology, natural science and astronomy broadened my mind, and most importantly, helped me find myself.

The overall consequence is that I came to believe I am a good person as I try hard to live by the moral values I was taught in my youth. These are indelibly etched on my mind and it was tearing them to shreds over and over again in my drugging days that had destroyed my self-esteem. (Today fear and self-centeredness sometimes cause me to forget, which is worse when I am tired or sick, and then little things can send my faith flying like dandelion seeds in the wind.)

But as soon as I apply the tools AA and NA point me towards, my attitude changes. The most accessible are prayer and my gratitude list, which quickly lift my thoughts out of the doldrums to which they have gravitated, and I am reminded of the permanent gifts of faith, love and freedom with which I have been blessed. So, from hating myself and life, the accumulation of the many good things I have received nurture my mind and soul back to feeling serene. It is as if I have been on a magic carpet ride and the overall effect is that I have come to love myself.

My conclusion is that the greatest gift I have received is a belief that a Higher Power – '*God as I understand Him*' – looks after me and, He, She or It always will.

By the time I was three years sober my wife and I were financially secure. We were amply supported by proceeds from her deceased father's estate, and I had a good income honestly earned from stockbroking. From witnessing others who were further advanced than me on a spiritual path but who had less materially, I came to understand that whatever I had moneywise was not as important as following the path, nor was my recovery from alcoholism and drug addiction dependent on how much I had in the bank. (I also knew at a very deep level that one drink or drug would set off a chain reaction over which I would have no control and everything I had would be lost forever.)

As I reflected on these facts it dawned on me that God's gifts had to be free and available to everyone, everywhere in the world. I also grasped that only I could apply the actions for my continuing spiritual growth, and for this God would always provide all the necessary means.

To improve my spiritual development further, I started to attend our local Hampstead church. Here I met the Reverend Gerry Moate, its newly appointed vicar. I will never forget what Gerry did for me, and his role in guiding me at this time. He was always kind and patient with me, spending hours sharing experiences of his life before he became a clergyman, some of which were so helpful to my accepting the sins of my own past as to endear him to me forever. Not that he had ever done anything as terribly wrong as I had.

After one of our meetings he said, 'There is a church in the City that has a service every Tuesday lunch time that I would like to take you to.'

We went there together the following week. It was very crowded. There were many ushers, all very helpful and polite. I discovered that due to the church's popularity another service followed immediately after; in total, I was told, about 1,000 people attended each week. It was the first time in my life that I had encountered such enthusiasm for religion, especially Christianity, which I had understood to be waning in most parts of Britain.

The church was St Margaret's, Lothbury, and it was here that I first heard about John Collins, vicar of Holy Trinity, Brompton – 'HTB'. Gerry suggested I contact him to ask if he and I could meet. I rang, and he said he would be delighted to see me the following Tuesday and invited me to his home for tea.

John was very kind as well. We met every week for over a year at his home in South Kensington on Tuesday evenings straight after I finished work. I would talk about my history of alcohol and drug abuse and where it had taken me to in life. I dotted the is and crossed the ts over the most sordid aspects, knowing that honesty was from now on was my only way forward. He never once blanched, judged me or put me down. His time freely given I will remember for as long as I live. Sometimes we would discuss passages from the bible, but mostly it was free and easy with no agenda. He also talked about the life of Christ and what it meant to him: he never once tried to convert me. He even let me bring my wife to meet him and his wife for tea, which I considered a most hospitable thing to do, given their immensely busy lives. At this time I still did not think I was worthy of such friendship and hospitality.

What impressed me most about John was something I found out after we stopped meeting. I had no idea at the time of the stature of HTB or its role in the creation of the worldwide acclaimed 'Alpha' course. Never did he try to persuade me to attend HTB or even to take the course. It was as if he knew I was on my own spiritual path and that he should let my 'Higher Power' guide me; after all, it had done pretty well so far!

Sometime later I did attend three HTB services taken by Sandy Millar and I also met their renowned preacher, Nicky Gumble. I could see why they were so popular, but I found at that time on my journey their way did not seem quite right for me, and John, I guess, had realised this may be the case too.

A few years further on I heard about one of HTB's well-known supporters, Jackie Pullinger, when I saw a documentary about her on television called *Chasing the Dragon*. Jackie is famous for her work in Hong Kong with heroin and opium addicts. In 1993 I visited her centre, The Hang Fook Camp, which used to be in the infamous 'walled city', home to the notorious Hong Kong Triad gangs; probably the most dangerous place on earth to be alone at night at that time.

When Jackie had first gone to Hong Kong alone as a young woman in her twenties, she had lived and worked with the worst of the addicts, criminals and prostitutes. She did not speak a word of Cantonese, the local Chinese dialect, and Christianity was the last thing on the minds of those who lived there. Due to her own deep faith in God and living life through Jesus Christ she had put up with the conditions until such time as the walled city was knocked down in the early nineties. By then, using the simple but effective formula of love and prayer, she had shown many of the most hardened drug addicts, criminals and prostitutes how to kick their habit, and also how to change their lives.

When I visited her clinic, I was able to see at first hand the wonders of the work she, or God as I now understood Him, had done. An account of her ministry appears in her books, *Chasing the Dragon* and *Crack in the Wall*, both of which give accounts of her faith and incredible courage. And if any reader has any doubts as to the results of her teachings or her amazing story, they too can visit her treatment facility just as I did. Because once I had been there I realised the results of her endeavours could not be refuted as she only had successes with everyone who followed her seemingly divinely-inspired directions.

When I added this to my first-hand experiences in London and other parts of the UK, Wales, Scotland, Ireland, France, Italy, Switzerland, Spain, Denmark, Portugal, Austria, Greece, Croatia, Germany, Israel, Egypt, UAE,

Iran, Iraq, Iceland, Bermuda, USA, Canada, Russia, Morocco, Algeria, India, China, Brazil, Mauritius, Australia, New Zealand and Caribbean islands, where I had contact with hundreds of thousands of alcoholics and drug addicts who had found permanent freedom from their addictions by praying to a power greater than themselves, my faith in *God of my understanding* grew, knowing there were no geographical or denominational boundaries.

In fact, I now know there are three and a half million former addicts and alcoholics who have taken the same approach and recovered all over the world whatever their religion, spiritual or non-beliefs, be these Hinduism, Buddhism, Islam, Judaism, Christianity, atheism or any other. All of which helped me come to know there is a wondrous 'force', 'spirit' or 'Higher Power' available to any human being who makes tapping into it their foremost priority. But because 'It' resides in the silent, invisible, infinite, eternal, it is often impossible to convince those who have not tried it to think otherwise; sadly, they condemn it without prior investigation.

To begin with I was like that, but I reached a point of such desperation in my life after everything else failed that the terror of dying forced me to blindly reach out to 'It'; by Amazing Grace, it has worked for me ever since.

****

Footnote. I received the gifts of living and faith described in this chapter because I applied the Twelve Steps of recovery programmes of AA and NA in every aspect of my life. In my thirty-five years' experience this has always been the result when any alcoholic or addict does the same.

Chapter 11

The Twelve Steps of Recovery

The Twelve Steps of recovery programmes of AA and NA can achieve total abstinence from all mood-altering chemicals if they are practised by any alcoholic or drug addict who has the desire to quit. The continued application of the simple principles they contain will also enable such an individual to remain drug free for the rest of their lives.

In my experience, and that of the millions of others who followed this formula, there are no exceptions: so, there should be no debate as to whether AA and NA work. It therefore makes sense that their recovery programmes be endorsed by governments and medical practitioners, and made available to every suffering alcoholic and drug addict all over the world.

There are of course those who have attended AA and NA who will say this is not the case. But on examination it will be found in every instance that such individuals will not have followed the suggestions made by those passing on the programmes' message of recovery. For six months I did exactly that. But my near-death hospital experience changed my attitude to what was being suggested by AA and NA members, and from then on, I did what I was told.

In other words, their programme started to work as soon as I admitted I was powerless over the influence of the prescription drugs and alcohol I consumed daily, I also needed to admit that my life had become unmanageable due to the problems I had with the police, finance, health, sex, my wife and family and was the reason I was out of work; after the initial challenge this caused my ego, surrendering and following those who had recovered suggestions became easy.

Step 1: *We admitted we were powerless over alcohol; that our lives had become unmanageable.*

Having acknowledged these facts to my sponsor – in my case a man who had been clean and sober six years – he suggested that for the next few months I read some AA/NA recovery literature and telephone him every morning, pray for a clean and sober day, write or read a gratitude list and go to as many AA or NA meetings as possible. Once I had been doing this for nearly two months, he told me I had taken Step 1.

Step 2*: Came to believe that a Power greater than ourselves could restore us to sanity.*

A few days later I had an argument with my wife. My sponsor's response was that from now on, whenever a person upset me, I was to pray for their, health, wealth and happiness. He added that if it was a circumstance or set of circumstances, I should say AA and NA's much-loved Serenity Prayer. As this was said at the end of every meeting, by now I knew it by heart.

> 'God grant me the serenity to accept the things I cannot change,
>   Courage to change the things I can,
>   And wisdom to know the difference.'

Step 3*: Made a decision to turn our will and lives over to the care of God **as we understood him.***

'Read the AA and NA literature on this subject and say the Step 3 prayer every morning until you know it by heart. After that keep saying it every day for the rest of your life,' was his advice this time.

> 'God, I offer myself to thee to build with me and do with me as thou wilt.
>   Relieve me of the bondage of self that I may better do thy will.
> Take away my difficulties that victory over them may bear witness to those I would help of thy power, thy love and thy way of life.'

A few weeks later my sponsor told me to read the suggestions for taking Step 4. He said that a detailed description of how to do it was contained in two books in both fellowships: they are *Alcoholics Anonymous* and *The Twelve Steps and Twelve Traditions* in AA, and *The Basic Text* and *It Works; How and Why?* in NA.

Step 4*: Made a searching and fearless moral inventory of ourselves.*

The most fundamental aspect of this written exercise was that it meant for the first time in my life I had to be honest about my past, and by doing so I would find the humility necessary to work through this and the remaining steps. (Before this time, I did not have even a nodding acquaintance with humility, always believing it was an unmanly failing!) Now it meant that in black and white I could see the stark reality of my problems and that they were *all* brought about by *me* and exacerbated by *my* self-centered shortcomings: especially fear, resentment, pride and dishonesty.

However, what a breakthrough this step was and for the first time in my life I joined the human race.

To remove once and for all the many secrets I had bottled up over the first forty years of my life, I was told I now needed to admit my wrongdoings and defects of character to my sponsor or another man such as a clergyman or doctor whom I could trust. I chose my sponsor.

Step 5: *Admitted to God, to ourselves and to another human being the exact nature of our wrongs.*

What a relief doing this was. After five two-and-a-half-hour sessions in my sponsor's home I finished sharing with him all the problems from my past. Here was a man who was twelve years sober and much respected inside and outside AA and NA. By his sharing back with me similar experiences of some of the bad things he had done in his alcoholic years, and never judging me, by the time we finished I was no longer shackled to my previous sins. I felt that heavy weights had been lifted off my shoulders and I was even redeemed. From that day on I went forward a free man.

Around this time one of my favorite daily readings was *God at Eventide* by The Two Listeners. When a few days later on 5th April 1987 I read the following, my redemption seemed absolute; I thought for the first time that maybe my life had a purpose:

Redemption

Agony & heartache, pain & loneliness, such as no human being has ever known, were the price of your redemption.

Truly you are not your own, bought with a price you belong to me,

You are mine to use, mine to love, mine to provide for.

Man does not understand the infinite Love of the Divine.

Man teaches that as I bought him, so he has to serve, obey & live for Me.

He fails to understand that because he is Mine, bought by Me,

It is My responsibility to supply your every need,

Your part is to realise My ownership and claim My love and power.

But I was getting ahead of myself. A few days later fear knocked me sideways when I received an unexpected tax bill and discovered I had badly swollen, bleeding haemorrhoids. Financial insecurity and fear of death were back and almost as bad as ever.

Fortunately, by now I knew what to do. I rang my sponsor and told him. His answer was immediate. He seemed to expect a call along these lines and more or less what I would say.

'Jack, it's time for Steps 6 and 7, two of the most important in the programme. First read the information about them in the literature; then every time fear arises, get on your knees and pray for it to be removed, just as you do every morning for your drug addiction and alcoholism.'

As soon as we hung up that was what I did. Since then I have prayed every time similar fears or resentments have surfaced and this approach to remove them has worked; though it has often needed to be done more than once, and for the more serious, many times.

Step 6: *Were entirely ready to have God remove all these defects of character.*

Step 7: *Humbly asked Him to remove our shortcomings*

Not long after, my sponsor told me the next stage in my recovery was to look at my Step 4 inventory and make a list of the people I had harmed, shops I had stolen from and companies from whom I made dishonest expense claims. He explained that I then needed to be willing to make restitution to each of these wherever possible and that doing so would unburden me of the wrongdoings of my past. As time has gone by since, I have come to realise it also peeled away the layers of self-hatred that had built up in my drug-using years. Again, he told me to read the relevant literature which would help guide me through this exercise.

Step 8: *Made a list of all persons we had harmed, and became willing to make amends to them all.*

Step 9: *Made direct amends to such people wherever possible, except when to do so would injure them or others.*

My amends fell into several categories. The more serious were to my family as I had neglected them badly in the last years of my alcohol and drug abuse. I had also been a mischievous, dishonest brat at times, which caused anguish to my parents, sister and teachers.

There were also instances of stealing from shops that had since closed and cheating on company expenses, totalling at least £4,000. Where I could, I repaid it and the balance I gave to charities based on 10% of my income after tax. (Although I have repaid the amounts I stole several times over. Having studied Islam, I continue to do this as I find the act of giving therapeutic.)

There was also my recently wed wife and several former girlfriends to atone to. In each instance, except for one who was French and may not have fully understood what I was saying, my reparations were well received.

The net result was that the guilt of my past with regard to each of these issues was layer by layer lifted. At the outset this had seemed daunting, but in the next few years making these amends produced the results AA predicts after Step 9 in what it calls The Twelve Promises:

(1)   *We are going to know a new freedom and a new happiness.*

(2)   *We will not regret the past nor wish to shut the door on it.*

(3)   *We will comprehend the word serenity and we will know peace.*

(4)   *No matter how far down the scale we have gone, we will see how our experience can benefit others.*

(5)   *That feeling of uselessness and self-pity will disappear.*

(6)   *We will lose interest in selfish things and gain interest in our fellows.*

(7)   *Self-seeking will slip away.*

(8)   *Our whole attitude and outlook upon life will change.*

(9)   *Fear of people and of economic insecurity will leave us.*

(10) *We will intuitively know how to handle situations which used to baffle us.*

(11) *We will suddenly realise that God is doing for us what we could not do for ourselves.*

(12) *Are these extravagant promises? We think not. They are being fulfilled among us – sometimes quickly, sometimes slowly. They will always materialise if we work for them.*

If someone had told me that by the end of the second year of my recovery these benefits would have accrued, I would have thought them totally insane. But they are exactly what happened, and most important of all, I had stayed clean and sober.

How to keep it this way is the purpose of the three remaining steps of the AA and NA programmes.

Step 10: *Continued to take personal inventory and when we were wrong promptly admitted it.*

Since taking this step I have taken an inventory of my life and behaviour daily and annually. When a difficulty arises, I do a spot check of my role in it. If it is a person that has caused me a problem, I pray for them, and if it is a situation, I say the Serenity Prayer. Just before going to sleep I do a review of any resentment, fears and self-centredness, mentally noting what I have done well. If there is bad resentment, I write it down and look at the cause. Then I revert to Step 7 and pray to my Higher Power to remove it. The result of these exercises is that as the years have gone by the negatives have diminished and the positives multiplied.

Once a year I go away by myself to review the past twelve months, as well as my life since my recovery began. What this does is make me see that as my problems have become fewer my gratitude for who I am, and my life today has grown.

Step 11: *Sought through prayer and meditation to improve our conscious contact with God **as we understood Him** praying only for knowledge of His will for us and the power to carry that out.*

To fill in the cracks in my faith that still appeared I applied the principles of more prayer and practice of daily meditation suggested in this step. My prayer life had begun with a simple request for a clean and sober day and evolved from there. In the ensuing months I added other prayers I liked contained in the AA and NA programmes. My meditations began in the second year of my recovery. To begin with they were short and several times a day, then grew longer and at least twice a day. Today, both prayer and meditation are essential in my life in much the same way as eating, breathing and sleeping.

One of the most important ways in which I combine both disciplines is the **St Francis Prayer.** Praying for what it contains in the first section and meditating on its selfless direction for living in the second means that in the years I have been doing it my attitude to life has changed:

> Lord, make me an instrument of your peace,
> Where there is hatred, let me sow love,
> Where there is injury, pardon,
> Where there is doubt, faith,
> Where there is despair, hope,
> Where there is darkness, light,
> And where there is sadness, joy,
> O, Divine Master, grant that I may not so much seek to be consoled
> as to console,
> To be understood, as to understand,

To be loved, as to love.
For it is in giving that we receive,
It is in pardoning that we are pardoned,
It is in self-forgetting that we find,
And in dying that we are born to Eternal Life.

Step 12: *Having had a spiritual awakening as the result of these steps, we tried to carry this message to alcoholics, and to practise these principles in all our affairs.*

It was teaching me how to live a drug-free life where the AA and NA programmes really scored. Not only have I had a life of abundance and joy these past thirty-five years, but my family life improved beyond measure. I do work which fits my interests and abilities like a glove, my interests have educated me in ways I could not have imagined, and I have come to believe that the *God of my understanding* takes care of me under all circumstances.

I also learned from Step 12 that service to others, charity, humility and forgiveness are essential ingredients to life, and the accumulated benefits of practising these principles each day bless my tomorrows – as opposed to the daily harrowing inputs I made in my drugging yesteryears. Clearly the former is better than the latter from both a personal and community point of view, but because of my former drug-influenced view, I was too blinkered to see this.

The results of such actions helped me develop reasonable self-esteem, as has the knock-on effect of being accepted by the people I have in my life today. Some of them had disassociated themselves from me previously for very good reasons.

My self-esteem was helped, too, by my creating a successful mergers and acquisitions business. I did business with people whom I used to revere; in fact, I would have been afraid to even to talk to them in bygone years: the chairmen and chief executives of public companies, City of London institutional fund and private equity managers, lawyers, accountants, investment bankers, stock brokers and investment analysts.

As my confidence grew, if it seemed appropriate, I told some of them I had once had an alcohol and drug problem. None of them batted an eyelid and often told me of relatives or friends with similar problems: two of them even asked for my help with their drinking problem and one came to an AA meeting with me. The support I always got from these people was much appreciated and meant I could be open and not hide important facts about myself. Everybody knows someone who has a drink or drug problem. Hiding mine would not help anyone, including me. Though to write my part of this book and protect AA and NA, I needed to do so using a pseudonym, as did the rest of the authors.

Chapter 12

Came to Believe

My faith in God has at times been tenuous and often I needed reassurance that He, She or It does exist. Believing in an invisible, incomprehensible, enigmatic Higher Intelligence when life was tough sometimes seemed beyond my human reach. But I now believe that because each time this happened, I blindly practised the appropriate spiritual tools; I was given what I needed to stay on my spiritual path. (This I only did because I had nowhere else to turn and for me today, I believe this is how God works: after all, I made my first cry for help when I was completely helpless and literally at death's door.)

In addition to prayer and meditation, the building of my faith mostly came from studying world religions, the work and writing of spiritual masters and unexplainable coincidences, some of which were truly extraordinary. (Coincidences are God's way of remaining anonymous. – Albert Einstein)

I was a few months sober and driving home from an AA meeting in Chelsea. For some reason unbeknown to me, I had over several days fallen into a most horrendous depression. My mind had become enveloped in a despairing hopelessness as to what future life had in store for me. It was so surreptitious in its approach that I had not been aware of it; sometimes I was teetering on its brink, at others I was in the midst of a deep dark cavern.

At that moment it was the bleakest I had ever been in. In every direction I looked the outlook was jet black and I knew there was nothing I could do about it. Needless to say, I was close to the jumping-off point, but I also knew that any form of mood-altering substance would make matters worse. I kept asking myself, 'What is the point of being alive? I am crap, I always have been crap, life is crap, I am going nowhere and there is no way out.'

I was passing Marble Arch's red-light district where I'd had dalliances with prostitutes in the past. I was desperate and wondered if one would fix me. At the same time, I was trying to say the Serenity prayer, which I now knew by heart. I must have said it at least a dozen times and eventually I said it out loud, then louder and louder.

I had the Peter Gabriel album *So* playing in the background, though I was unaware I was listening to it. All of a sudden, the words of his classic song *Don't Give Up* with Kate Bush singing them filled my ears. These resonated perfectly with my thinking; they changed my life forever:

I will never forget the healing impact these words had on me. The line *'Don't give up'* was repeated many times and as I absorbed its timing and meaning, my depression started to lift. By the time I reached home I felt totally different. I knew I was safe, and the future would get better from here on.

Over the next few years, I had several similar depressions, but none lasted as long. On each occasion I always knew they would pass and that was the case. A few Serenity prayers and sometime soon after I would be on the other side in bright sunshine. It was as if I were peeling off layers of my naturally negative past thinking to let new light in.

I was told *'There is no growth without pain'*, and as a result of my experiences, I can vouch for this. Today I am convinced that all my painful episodes were necessary and 'provided' to help my faith develop; that way I learned I had to apply spiritual tools to pull me through, and practice makes perfect. Now I believe this was my Higher Power at work, though knowing how much I hate pain and difficulties, He, She or It should have checked with me first!

In the next two years an extraordinary trail of coincidences took place in my life. Most I cannot remember, but at the time each helped reinforce my belief that a Higher Power was taking care of me. There was at least one instance most weeks and I had the impression they were God's way of revealing Himself. Whether my interpretation was right or wrong does not matter, to me it was correct as I knew I was the only one on my precise path and this was the way my Higher Power chose to guide me. I also knew no one else had arrived at the start of their journey in the same way I had, which helped to prevent me questioning the spiritual journeys of my peers who walked very different paths.

The most mindboggling coincidence of all took place one Friday night on my way to a dinner party at my friend Steve's place. My wife and I had just left home by car, and she asked me what I was planning to do the next day. I had not got a clue. Suddenly I remembered it was the FA Cup Final; Wimbledon were playing Liverpool.

'I'm probably going to watch the Cup Final in the afternoon,' I answered, wanting to give the impression I was busy in case she was considering other plans for me! She did not reply.

At this time, I often occupied my mind while driving playing games with car registration numbers. I would figure out words or expressions from the combinations of their letters. As the words spilled out of my mouth the very next car had as its first three letters 'WNR'.

I immediately translated this as 'WiNneR'.

The next car had the letters 'WMN' – WiMbledoN!

I could not believe it!

When the very next car's was 'WBD'; again WimBleDon and the one immediately after 'WNS' – 'WiNS' I almost drove into it!

I sat bolt upright, afraid to say anything. I knew from my considerable experience of studying British car number plates that each of these combinations was unusual, and to have them appear on consecutive cars was bordering on the statistically impossible; yet there they were, one immediately after the other with no gaps in between.

I knew if Wimbledon won, they would be the biggest outsiders to win for years and wondered, if this truly was a divinely-inspired message, should I place a big bet?

I said nothing at dinner, believing everyone would think I was stark raving mad if I told my story. I did not even tell my wife until we were on our way home. She was tired and nonplussed, so I dropped the subject.

Whether or not these coincidences were Higher Power-led I will never actually know. However, what I do know is that I would not have put money on the outcome, or so much, if I had not taken the view it might be. Today I have no qualms about anyone thinking my thoughts insane, but if this happened to you, what would you do?

Next day I awoke wondering what to do. I was a little nervous and excited, but determined to put a big bet on Wimbledon to win. I was struggling to determine how much when I went into a betting shop in Marloes Road in Kensington. The odds on their blackboard enticed me to bet even more than I had planned. My Herefordshire Constabulary police number was 114, and Wimbledon were 11/4. I immediately knew how much to put on: £114!

Less than an hour later I was watching the match at Campden Hill Tennis Club with some friends. Again, I said nothing. When Wimbledon scored, I nearly fell off my chair with excitement. I spent every second of the rest of the match with my nerves on edge and the final few minutes dragged forever. Then the final whistle and Wimbledon had won! I leapt with joy and was soon off to the betting shop to collect my winnings, wishing, of course, I had bet much more!

Steve, the party-giver, gambled in a big way in stocks and shares, so next time I saw him I shared my experience. He replied, 'I wish you had told me. I would have bet my shirt on Wimbledon. It would be like receiving inside information in the stock market.'

Hmm, I thought, let's just hope it happens again. But sadly, it has not!

At two years sober my faith was still up and down but had strengthened all the time. To take me forward, almost as if out-of-the-blue I started to see crosses, the same as the symbol used in Christianity. I could be almost anywhere and if I felt fear or anger creeping into my emotions, I would see a cross. The cross was usually made by panels in a wooden door, the intersections of a window frame, beams on a ceiling, or joins in floor or wall tiles. Never did I try to create them; they would just appear. I found them a great comfort on many occasions, and they gave me the courage to go on. This was especially true when I was worried about something such as operations in hospitals, dental surgery or having to speak my mind when fearful of the outcome. Today I still see them, but now they are part of my everyday life, and always they are reassuring.

I had always been terrified of flying and used Valium and alcohol to give me Dutch courage in the past. The first time I flew in recovery, as I mounted the steps to the plane my fears came flooding back. Immediately I started repeating the Serenity prayer. Suddenly there, by the passenger door, where sheets of metal joined, was the perfect Christian-style cross. My fears evaporated, for I believed my Higher Power (HP) was already on board. On the hundreds of occasions I have flown since, not once has my fear of flying returned with any significant force.

There were two occasions when I had the belief my HP had arrived at my destination before me. The first was on a visit to Dallas on an American Airlines plane. Immediately on disembarking there was a huge sign, 'AA welcomes you to the USA' Yes, I did feel welcome! The second was on a holiday to Brazil with my wife. I was three years sober and nervous about being away from my regular London surroundings. We were staying in Manaus, the old Portuguese city in the heart of the Amazon jungle. Nerves jangling, as I knew there were no AA or NA meetings there, I went outside the airport concourse to get a taxi. Immediately my mind was at ease: every car had the registration letters AA! From that moment on I believed I was as safe in this isolated place as any I could visit on the planet.

****

It maybe that some readers have begun to think I should be in a mental institution. If you are one of those, please remember, this is my story and this has worked to keep me alcohol and drug free for thirty-five years, the only real objective in my life. I am a great believer in the adage, *'If it works don't fix it.'*

****

I was given my biggest spiritual boost of all in a dream. Although the incidents that followed did not provide me with a clear-cut certainty that I had my very own guardian angel, they were sufficient for me to think that maybe I had. Their timing, and the way they had built up, coupled with my many other coincidences, and seeing crosses, were enough to convince me this actually was the case.

When I was in my early teens my father watched me nearly drown. He stood on Glasbury Bridge, helplessly looking down into the River Wye below in a state of sheer panic. On this occasion some friends swimming nearby rescued me.

I was one of three children and my eldest sister had died from a fall several years earlier; consequently, my father's fear must have been horrendous.

In my third year of recovery from alcoholism, I dreamt about it. This time I was lifted from the water and slowly rose, following a few strides behind a figure wearing a white full-length gown. After a few moments he turned and looked at me. It was a man with the image of the most commonly-held impression of Jesus Christ – about thirty years old, long, dark flowing hair, beard and gentle face. After we had risen about fifty metres, I was gently set down on a nearby riverbank, together with two suitcases I was carrying.

At that point I awoke. Within an instant, running through my mind were words from the Leonard Cohen song *Suzanne*. After subconsciously repeating lines I remembered from it several times, I got up and went downstairs.

For a few minutes I stood motionless, gazing through a window at the night sky, playing over and over again these same words in my head. It was then I remembered other lines, and these caused me to become fully awake.

Now my brain was fully concentrated on these incredible 'messages'. In much amazement I concluded that here was the evidence of Providence I had unknowingly always sought: I had a guardian angel looking after me and that had been the case even in my darkest hours.

I could hardly believe it, but come to believe it I did. These were facts, and although they emanated from the surreal, 'I' had not created them. They were as real as the leaves on the trees and the birds of the air I loved so much. I felt good about them and that was all I needed to know.

As I reflected later, I realised the method of revelation was in line with the modus operandi I had come to expect from the guiding light I had so recently found in my subconscious: subtle, but once the layers of doubt were lifted, almost obvious. The same 'fingerprints', I had started to see, were everywhere, but close-mindedness, arrogance and not knowing how or where to look had dogged my every step before. Now open-mindedness, humility and an honest desire to try to find God had led me to this point on my spiritual path; our game of hide-and-seek was over.

I have never forgotten either the dream or the words of the song and have often recalled them since at low times in my life. I saw that I'd had a gradual spiritual awakening and I had also been blessed with a profound spiritual experience. I came to believe that this was the easy-to-see start of my resurrection and that I was then, and have been since, looked after by my Heavenly Father.

I have since come to interpret my dream as the gift of a second chance and that the suitcases contained all the experiences from my former life. My being put back on earth again meant I was given all I would need to live out the rest of my life and at the same time I was to pass on this message to others, especially no-hoper alcoholics and addicts. Though what the suitcases really contained I do not know, nor will I ever know if my dream interpretation was correct. But what does that matter, as I reflect upon the impact it had on me and the life I have been blessed with since?

Looking back further, I now believe that my life had always been one of preparation for where I am at precisely today. In my first forty-five years (including five clean and sober) I had spent time in Northern Ireland, South Africa, India, Israel, the USA and Yugoslavia, and when the racial, ethnic or religious troubles arose in each, I found it useful to reflect from first-hand experience upon those things I had witnessed in each of these countries.

Also, the time I had spent working in the British police's Criminal Investigation Department gave me insights into legal and criminal procedure, which I could also apply to my reflections, especially with crimes associated with drugs.

Adding these experiences to my more recent studies of the teachings and practices of the world's major religions and philosophy, plus what I had learned from my examinations of geology, astronomy, natural history and science, helped me come to believe that there is a presiding, all-powerful Creator of all there is, ever has been and always will be. And even though some of His, Her or Its methods did not make sense to me, I came to believe their plan must be that one day all mankind will live in peace and harmony: though how we get to that time is for Him, Her or It to decide, not me!

As I had never had worldly views before, and certainly none of a positive kind, I was somewhat surprised to arrive at such a philosophical conclusion. Today, a smile comes over my face every time I muse on the progress I have made and marvel that a spiritual awakening should have happened to a former bum like me.

Since embarking upon my new way of life it has always seemed as though I was being led rather than charting my own course – not 'my way' anymore. Either I would be introduced to a new book or guru, or I would receive some new idea or revelation to help my understanding. These revelations would often come from a totally unexpected source. Therefore, I learned to listen to everyone I met just in case they were the next link in my spiritual chain of development. The sources were people I talked to at dinner and cocktail parties, new and old friends, airline and train passengers, taxi drivers and others who briefly entered my life. It seemed as though as long as I stayed open-minded and aware of this notion, I was being led, the instructions would naturally flow.

Often the facts of nature I unearthed, and my interpretations, seemed quite bizarre, yet always they were exquisitely timed, while sometimes they reinforced what I already knew. I recalled again the expression, 'When the student is ready the teacher appears'. Every such encounter seemed to happen at precisely the right time, not a second too soon, or a minute, hour or day too late.

In my various homes I frequently encountered spiders. Often this happened when I was going through a difficulty in my life which made me want to give up, so I used the story of Robert Bruce and the spider to get me through.

It was said that in the early days of his reign he was defeated by the English and driven into exile. He sought refuge in a cave and his pastime was watching a spider make a web. Over and over again the spider would fall and have to climb back up. After many attempts the spider managed to stick a strand of silk to the cave wall and was then able to weave a web. This inspired Bruce to return to the fray and defeat the English at Bannockburn.

The moral to me of this was always, 'If at first you don't succeed, try, try, and try again.'

One of my most astonishing coincidental encounters occurred on a flight between Denver and Los Angeles. I was in the middle of a ski holiday in

Breckenridge, Colorado with my son. Just before leaving England I had read a Deepak Chopra book that made references to Merlin the magician. Due to my Welsh heritage and enthusiasm for spiritual enlightenment, I had made endeavours in local bookshops and libraries to study Merlin's wizardry further. I had not found it easy and came up with very little.

I was halfway through the flight when lunch was served. Many times in the recent past I had used this time to start a conversation with my passenger neighbour. I had glanced at the man sitting next to me once or twice but not found him too inspiring; he seemed to be reading a children's book!

After debating in my head whether to speak or not I finally said, 'Hello. I was wondering what you are reading?'

He laughed and closed the book so that I could not see the cover. Then he said with seeming embarrassment, 'It's a children's book. As I was leaving home, I just grabbed it as I went through the door. It's one of my twelve-year-old son's school reading books.'

I said, 'Is it any good?'

Again, he laughed and said, 'Yes, it's quite interesting. It's the story of a magician called Merlin.'

I could not believe it!

I said, 'You may not believe this, but I have been hunting high and low in England for information about the history of Merlin and not come up with anything worthwhile. Do you mind if I have a look at it?'

It transpired his son's book contained all I needed to know about Merlin. The moral of this story for me was, 'Never judge a book by its cover!'

Since then I have seldom held back in opening conversations with strangers who have been put in my path, though one or two taxi drivers were not quite as enlightening as my American co-passenger!

This meeting was just one of many instances along these lines. There were numerous others, all of which added to my spiritual growth. One of the most interesting was meeting Jo, who gave me numerous similar introductions to authors and an anthologist with whose works I was unfamiliar.

Jo had been on her own spiritual path for many years and was a great fan of Carlos Castaneda and Joseph Campbell. But it was when she introduced me to Dostoyevsky's *Diary of a Writer* that my spiritual journey went forward in leaps and bounds. Reading his dream about 'paradise' where everyone lived in harmony, after my own dream experience, and my already being a fan of Sir Thomas More's idea of Utopia, left me with an almost certain belief that such a 'paradise' or 'Utopia' was precisely what God has in store for the people of planet Earth. What other divine purpose could there be? I reasoned.

One other major occurrence had a profound influence on my early spiritual development. When I had been drug-free for about two years I went on a two-week business trip to several European cities. In the middle weekend I decided to make a social visit to Venice rather than return to London. I had visited Venice once, seven years previously, with a friend, Vicky, on the first of my many attempts to stop drinking. This had failed miserably and I remembered little of the weekend, except that much of it was yet another unhappy drunken experience, most of which was in blackout. (Blackout is a condition familiar to alcoholics. It is a period of time - short or long - when they have no recollection of anything.)

Vicky was a doctor's daughter and I thought her father's medical influence might have rubbed off on her, and so help me find the strength I needed to quit the by-now dreaded booze. Little did I realise then that no other person could help solve my addiction problem: it had to be an inside job, I had to find the willingness and strength within me to conquer my overwhelming need for alcohol and drugs.

As my aeroplane was circling over the Venetian lagoon, I got out my previous trip's Venice guide. I had not opened it since that time, and inside, much to my surprise, I found an old black and white postcard, which was actually a photograph of the inside of a church called Santa Maria dei Miracoli.

As soon as I read its name, I became excited. I knew almost for certain that something special had happened to me there. I assumed the translation must be 'The Church of St Mary of the Miracle'.

Immediately after breakfast the next day, I found my way to the church and memories came flooding back. I remembered how Vicky had become angry with me because I had got drunk the previous night in Harry's Bar. She had left me sitting alone on the church steps. Wallowing in self-pity, I had started to cry. As my despair enveloped me more and more, I had lain down and ended up crying uncontrollably, realising for the first time in my life that I was completely beaten by alcohol and I was going to die from it as the result. I lay there for some fifteen minutes as this realisation grew deeper and deeper. I eventually got up, caught up with my friend, apologised, and spent the rest of the weekend drowning my sorrows and asking her to forgive my pathetic disposition.

Little did I know then that my *cri de coeur* was being heard and would be answered in full several years later, but that in the interim my situation would get considerably worse. Indeed, that my downhill progression had scarcely begun, for in front of me lay the worst five years that I could ever have imagined.

But that Santa Maria experience was then, and this was now. I then recapped on other instances where the name Maria had transpired to influence me. I recalled my encounter with the prostitute who called herself Santa Maria, and that on this, the second night I had met her, I was wining and dining with the one 'true love' of my life also, Maria. I then recalled how on my earlier skiing holiday to Switzerland, when I drank alcohol on Antabuse for the first time, that it was a 'Virgin Mary' I had been sipping! Although these were little things, they all added to my belief that I was being divinely led.

Until I got sober I had not realised the power of prayer, simply because I had never tried it: but the fear of an alcoholic and drug-induced death had changed that. For the past thirty five years I had used it to deal with my fears, difficulties and resentments; so in 2008 when I was diagnosed with throat cancer, as soon as I got home, where I lived alone, I got on my knees and prayed for the fear of dying to be lifted. Although it returned briefly on occasions before I had an operation to have the tumour removed, this action always worked for at least the next few hours. When I couple this with my prayers to release me from alcoholism and drug addiction, I need no further proof to know that prayer works.

When I first began to meditate, nothing much happened. To begin with sitting quietly for just a few minutes three or four times each day was difficult. After practising this for two years, the periods lengthened, and things started to happen: simple messages began to enter my mind. The most frequent were, and still are:

'It is My responsibility to provide your every need; your part is to realise My ownership and claim my love and power.'

'Learn to love yourself, trust yourself. Be who you are, not what you would like to be.'

'Wherever you go, whatever you do, I will be there.'

'Be kind and more loving than you have ever been.'

As I learned to meditate for longer periods, on numerous occasions there has been an unsolicited 'click' in my ears and instantly I would be enveloped in a much richer world of pure silence. At these times I seemed to be suspended in space and nothing could disturb me. I had found perfect peace.

But these are not the only times something like this happened. While writing these reflections I have been reminded that in my early teens, on hot summer days, I would sometimes lie by myself on a wall by a slow-running part of the River Wye. As the river meandered a few metres below, I would close my eyes and marvel at the tranquillity, beauty, and wonders of nature all around me: the warm gentle breeze drifting up from the river, the sounds of insects, sheep and cows in the meadows opposite, and occasionally a curlew or lapwings a few fields away.

At these times I also found serenity and peace, and with hindsight I realise they were some of the most precious moments I have known in my life. But being so young I did not fully appreciate them; at that time, I believed I had to be with friends or be active to be happy.

Whether these thoughts and sublime experiences are the nearest I ever get to God, I do not know; but as I look back on my life, I realise such moments are the memories I treasure most. Today, aged 76, as I contemplate my life going forward, all I want are as many more of the same as possible.

So, by sorting out my past, making amends where necessary, learning to pray and meditate, read spiritual literature, give to charity, and do service for others, I found a way of life that was preferable to any I had witnessed in my past pursuit of materialism. I also learned that every spiritual journey is individual, but that each of us can climb aboard at any time we plead for help. As I have seen this happen to thousands of others, who, after faltering steps like mine, once on board, had a spiritual awakening. As I had seen with Jacky Pullinger's opium addicts in Hong Kong, I now had my own proof that anyone who wishes to conquer their addiction to any form of drug needs to pray from the heart for help and the appropriate guidance will materialise.

The shame of it is that because of politicians' hypocritical drug laws and the medical profession's blinkeredness to alcoholism and drug addiction being an illness, it took me many years to find the peace I had found as a teenager on that wall by the River Wye in Glasbury. *But millions of others will not be so fortunate and die unless they change their policies and tell the truth: THAT RECOVERY FROM BOTH IS POSSIBLE AND THEY ARE SICK PEOPLE NOT CRIMINALS.*

Footnote:

In 2011 my 99-year-old mother, Kitty, went into a nursing home. For the next three years her mental faculties were as good as ever. She spent most days in a conservatory with her eyes closed or looking out of the window at passersby and traffic. All her life she had been an atheist or agnostic. She knew I had been a Quaker for over twenty years, yet in her 102nd year she gave me one of the most enlightening experiences of my life. Our conversation that memorable Sunday went something like this:

'Did you go to your Quaker meeting today?'

'Yes. As you know I like sitting in silence and the hour I have there centres me for the rest of the day.'

'I'm pleased for you. I wish I had done the same years ago. I only knew two Quakers and they were lovely people.'

'But you don't believe in God, so why would you want to have done that?'

After a long sigh, based on her three years of almost permanent reflection, with a smile on her face and light in both eyes, she answered, 'Oh, but I do now. It's the only thing that makes sense.'

There was nothing I could say. I had never been happier for my mother in my life.

As I wrote this on 10th April 2014, she was still going strong. On August 4th that year she passed from this world. But by then I knew she had died in peace.

****

Every night for many years I have kept a diary of all that I have seen and done that day that affected my mental state, both positively and negatively. In my early years of recovery there was much that was negative, but in the last twenty five my thoughts have been mostly positive. Once a year I isolate myself for a day to reflect on these and analyse what I find. The result is remarkable; what I find makes me realise that my life has got better every year.

I always conclude that I have been blessed spiritually and physically, and when I add my studies of the universe, the wonders of nature and evolution, I realise I have also been blessed mentally. But the most wondrous gift of all is that I have been given the opportunity to help others similarly afflicted with alcoholism and drug addiction, and as a result I have directly witnessed the recoveries of hundreds of thousands of members of Alcoholics Anonymous and Narcotics Anonymous. The icing on that cake is that there are millions more like us in the world today, and with the help of this book, my hope is that many of those will be equally blessed.

The rest of Part 2 of *Millions of Miracles* contains some of their stories.

The writers are addicts and alcoholics from a variety of social, cultural, sexual, religious and racial backgrounds who have recovered, meaning they are clean and sober today and have been for many years. There are also others who died after spending much of their lives addiction free and some of their stories can be found in the literature of Alcoholics Anonymous, Narcotics Anonymous, Al-Anon and other 12-Step Fellowships. It was their examples that are used to pass on the message of recovery today to the rest of the world.

If you have a wife or husband, son or daughter, brother or sister, mother or father, work colleague, or friend who has an alcohol, or any other drug or addiction problem we ask you to encourage them to read the stories that follow. The likelihood is they will find at least one that contains enough similarities to give them the hope and direction they need to become free of their disease, and from there on live a happy, meaningful life.

Chapter 13

David's Story – A medical man in more ways than one

'My name is David, and I am an alcoholic.' It was a strange experience hearing those words, particularly as I was the one who had just said them. Denial is everything to an actively addicted person, and for over thirty years I had refused to admit that I drank too much. But when I first stopped drinking and found myself in meetings with other alcoholics, I heard people talking about how they never felt a part of anything: their families, groups of friends, and work colleagues. I recognised this feeling of separation.

I had been told that I had a restless nature, which manifested itself as dissatisfaction and irritability. Well maybe that was true. Then there was the anger, frustration, resentment and fear that we alcoholics suffer from. One of the men I spoke to at AA said, 'We're just wired up the wrong way. I never had a sociable drink in my life. It was always to make me feel that I belonged, or to blot out the anxiety that gnawed away at me.' He also quoted a section from the *Big Book of Alcoholics Anonymous*, which stated that I would become happy, joyous and free. Surely that was asking a bit too much.

I was born in Birmingham in 1951 to a single girl of seventeen and adopted a few weeks later. My new parents, Derrick and Kathleen, were loving and determined to give me a good upbringing, while I was equally determined to get my own way in everything. For the next fifty years of my life I was certain that I knew what was best for me and the good advice of others was just an attempt to cramp my style. As I would find out in late middle age, I had plenty of ego and little humility.

I would describe my childhood as basically happy, but within me there was a strong undercurrent of anxiety and self-doubt, topped with a lack of self-confidence that grew worse as time passed. When I was five, my younger brother Donald was born, my parents' natural child. I resented the fact that he was actually theirs – flesh and blood, so to speak. I should add that I was never loved less than Don, always treated fairly, and that he and I now have a wonderful brotherly relationship.

Only once during my childhood did I admit that I was adopted because when I was growing up there was a stigma attached to illegitimacy that does not exist today. Unfortunately, it was to an eleven-year-old girl who lived down the road and she ran away shouting out that I was a bastard for all to hear. I was mortified. For weeks I lived in fear, certain that my dirty secret would be widely circulated, but fortunately nothing came of it. I mention this as one example of the extreme sensitivity that marked my young life and which continued long after I felt I should have grown out of it. In fact, I frequently looked at people whom I considered good adults and assumed that sooner or later I, too, would become like them. Little did I realise that I was not alone in these feelings. My AA sponsor told me that for much of his life he had felt like a juvenile trapped in a man's body. I heard other fellow alcoholics say that they felt like frightened little boys and identified strongly with this sentiment.

I was bright and hard-working at school, trying hard not to fail while at the same time doing my best to fit in with the bad crowd and avoid being labelled a swot. I always thought of myself as a chameleon: I would be whatever you wanted me to be as long as you liked me. I wanted to be edgy, risqué and a bit dangerous, the sort of kid others admired and feared in equal measure, but I really wasn't up to it.

I had my first drink on a school trip to Cromer and loved it, even though I had little recollection of the evening and felt very detached the next day. I discovered that I could rely on being served in the pubs of Leeds and felt totally at home in them. From my teens onwards, I frequently drank to blackout, although when I arrived in rehab years later, I still did not understand that blackout simply meant having little or no recall of the events of the evening before.

I studied medicine at university in London in the late sixties and early seventies where I became a hippy, flaunting my purple crushed velvet trousers and shoulder bag in lectures, to the despair of the more conventionally dressed students and staff. Heavy alcohol consumption was not exactly frowned upon in medical school and, when I combined the drink with the drugs that were an integral part of the psychedelic age, they accentuated the nervousness that I had always felt. It was only the responsibility of a life in medicine that held my drinking and soft drug consumption in check, and as time wore on I worked harder and harder, trying to minimise the time available for drinking so that I could at least do a good job and try to control my booze intake.

Early in my medical career I was prescribed diazepam for anxiety symptoms and as the years wore on I found it increasingly hard to do without it, so what was intended as a short-term prescription ended up being my companion for the next twenty-seven years. I always felt ashamed of my dependence on diazepam and rarely collected the prescriptions myself.

I married the love of my life, Jenny, in 1978 and together we had three wonderful sons, but the peace of mind that I sought through family and career was as elusive as ever. Jenny usually collected my prescriptions and I avoided requests from a number of family doctors to discuss what in hindsight was an obvious tranquilliser addiction.

I was increasingly filled with an impotent rage which usually had no obvious cause outside the stuff of daily family life, and I could not understand why my apparent success wasn't accompanied by the contentment I saw in others. I was a dedicated but arrogant doctor, frequently insufferable at home and increasingly reliant on tranquillisers to quell my feelings of dissociation and panic caused by my underlying state of anxiety. It was only in recovery that I began to realise that although my life had seemed like wading through cement, Jenny and my boys had usually found it harder.

Slowly it dawned on me that, ever since I was an apprehensive teenager, I had felt different from others, not readily accepted by them. It always felt as if I was standing outside a circle into which everyone else had ready access. Groucho Marx said that he would refuse to join any club which would have someone like him as a member! I was like Groucho; whenever I tried to join in something, I felt rejected. 'Treat me special and I feel average, treat me normal and I feel rejected,' was how one AA member put it, and that was me.

I could not understand why, despite being bright and determined to build a successful career, all my triumphs left me feeling empty. I sought satisfaction in lovers, pills and booze, and later in my work and with my wife and children, but it was elusive. I built an ego the size of the planet to hide behind but was never content.

My use of tranquillisers continued over the years, some prescribed and some taken from either my workplace or Jenny's (she worked at a veterinary surgeon's) when the opportunities presented themselves. Eventually my family doctor persuaded me to see an eminent psychiatrist and I was prescribed the antidepressant Seroxat to help me tail off diazepam, something that I predictably failed to do. In fact, I found that Seroxat was remarkably effective at lowering my stress levels and enabling me to tolerate more booze without suffering incapacitating hangovers. The combination of large amounts of alcohol combined with diazepam and Seroxat seemed to me to be ideal, but it distanced me further from reality and allowed me to develop the sort of behaviour that hastened my final descent into round-the-clock drinking.

I have since learned how common tranquilliser and antidepressant abuse is amongst alcoholics after they have been medically prescribed to treat their alcoholism. Because the drugs do not address the underlying condition and, as a medical professional, I know such treatment cannot work.

There is another phrase that was always very pertinent to my life, and that is 'deep down inside I am really very shallow'. If I don't think much of me, then how are others supposed to? So I created an exaggerated person for people to like, a super-successful professional with a happy family, a large house and two weeks by the pool in Tuscany each year for starters. Strangely, this also failed to bring the peace of mind I looked for, but there was always one thing that worked and that was pouring a bottle of alcohol down my throat at every opportunity.

In the addiction therapy programme I found myself in seventeen years ago, one of the counsellors used to say that I would be following a spiritual path in recovery and I realised that I had no idea what he meant since, as a drinking alcoholic, it had become enough to merely exist, to get through each day, and I had long since ceased to question and expand my horizons. On the contrary, my world had been steadily shrinking for a decade or more and all the joy and wonder in life had slowly been wrung out of it. There was no space for spiritual considerations.

In the treatment centre all patients were prescribed large doses of librium to smooth out transition to abstinence, together with large doses of vitamins. Four times a day we queued for handfuls of medication at a counter, a practice that reminded me of scenes from the film *One Flew Over the Cuckoo's Nest*. After I had completed my detox, I decided that I would stop taking diazepam and Seroxat. Thanks to controlled tapering off, this turned out to be reasonably straightforward, with insomnia the main side effect.

Once we had detoxed, we all had to write a life story – in my view a fairly useless exercise for a man only two weeks off the booze, tranquillisers and antidepressants, but I complied since, as always in my life, I was fearful of rejection if I failed to do what found favour with those I wished to think well of me. My story was the sad monologue of a bitter man who feels that his family, friends and colleagues have failed him. At no stage did it occur to me that some of it, (some of it? Come on, all of it!) could have been my fault. But it was. I had been standing in the shadows for too long. My thinking was completely screwed up and I was by now an empty shell, completely lacking all the spiritual attributes that sustain us in this life – humility, patience, courage, love, and tolerance – and enveloped by a massive ego.

I will never understand why today I am one of the fortunate ones rescued from the abyss, but I shall never stop being grateful to the Spirit of the Universe with which I connected on that dark dawn seventeen years ago and to my family and friends who supported me and did more than anyone has a right to expect.

Many alcoholics and drug addicts simply drink themselves to extinction. My brother still says from time to time that I must have incredible willpower. But I do not. I simply realised that I was powerless over my addictions and that I needed external help. For too long I had tried to run my life exactly the way I wanted, but that had caused me to become alienated from my family and friends, so by the time I turned up at the treatment centre and started attending AA meetings I felt very alone.

I have to admit that when I sat in the meeting rooms of Alcoholics Anonymous those first few weeks, I had a lot of trouble accepting expressions like 'Higher Power', but two things worried me most. Firstly, I had to be honest with people, and especially with my new mentor, or sponsor as they are called; and secondly, I would have to make amends to all those I had harmed.

To begin with this filled me with fear, but as I progressed and continued to follow the steps of the programme, my life began to alter. The changes were subtle to start with and when, after a few months, a fellow alcoholic told me one evening that I had changed dramatically from the person he had first encountered, I asked how. He simply said that I had been an arrogant, intolerable, and fearful man then, but now I was becoming more like a decent human being.

I made nearly all the amends that I identified with my sponsor's help and felt progressively more liberated each time I made one. Astonishingly, everyone forgave me, although many left me in no doubt as to how difficult I had been.

Importantly, I also forgave myself and I have tried to stop obsessing over what people think of me. This is not always easy as, despite appearances, addicts are sensitive souls; we don't give ourselves up easily! The low self-esteem that afflicts addicts remains with us for months or even years after putting down the bottle or pills, but this is a small problem when compared to the dark days of round-the-clock drinking and pill-popping. Most of all, I now always try to put others first and to be as helpful to them as possible.

It still amazes me how rich my life has become by following a few simple spiritual principles. I have been able to fill what I have heard described as 'the hole in the soul' and can now deal with life as I find it. It is not always easy, but I no longer medicate away those uncomfortable feelings, I listen to them and try to understand what they are telling me.

One day at a time it can be a beautiful life!

Chapter 14

Alice's Story – A Portuguese Connection

My name is Alice, and I am a drug addict and alcoholic. I was born and bred in Portugal. At the tender age of twenty-three, I left for England in pursuit of a solution for my heroin addiction. I am fifty-three years old now, which means that the second half of my life has had a heavy British influence.

I grew up in Lisbon in a middle-class family where life was easy and happy. Surrounded by close relatives and a wide circle of family friends, my childhood was spent reading, visiting museums and historical sites, holidaying abroad, going to the theatre and political demonstrations, eating out, etc. The weekends were filled with private parties at my parents' friends' houses and our beach house.

My apparently carefree existence was overshadowed by what I know now to be the chains of a progressive and incurable disease called addiction. I felt it from the moment I acquired some kind of consciousness about who I was and where I fitted in. I was special and different and belonged nowhere. Others' perception of me was in complete opposition to my own. So, I turned into an actor, a chameleon, a great pretender in order to fulfil their expectations, and at the same time hide my true identity, which was bad and mad in nature. With that persona fulfilled, I became normal and part of the human race, or so I thought. But abandoning my identity in order not to feel like an alien didn't work and ultimately I had to ravage my body with many substances before I found freedom. I possessed an unnatural sense of entitlement that made me feel superior and helped justify my off-the-wall behaviour.

The spiral started with insignificant thrills like eating chocolate, stealing and smoking cigarettes, but quickly progressed to tastier ones. Solvents were replaced by alcohol and hashish in no time, and at secondary school I got introduced to uppers and downers: Rohypnol (strong tranquilliser) and Mandrax (sedative/hypnotic) to get through the day and amphetamines (can't remember the name of the pills) to revise for tests at night. The only frustration was that my brain would go blank at crucial moments and I couldn't understand why, as I had spent three days studying and writing non-stop and could literally feel my mind expanding with the effects of this fantastic drug!

By the age of fourteen or fifteen, I was on a self-destructive path. I was groomed and abused by a close friend of my parents and felt like life was not worth living. To add insult to injury, I lived in constant fear this person was going to get me at any given time and I would not get away. So, instead, I let the terror in my head lead, and each time I got drunk or drugged, I became detached, so it did not matter because that way I did not care any longer.

A promiscuous stage ensued as I believed my body was the only thing anyone wanted or that was worth offering. Relationships with men were all sexual in nature and the ones I had with women were non-existent, apart from wardrobe swapping.

Cocaine was the next drug I tried, and I loved it. It allowed me to drink copious amounts of alcohol without throwing up or passing out; it also gave me a sharpness I did not know I possessed. There was only a small, unpleasant side-effect: it made me feel that my heart was going to pop out of my mouth. But like any other teenager, I believed I was immortal and heart attacks were not on my agenda of possibilities, so I persevered with a passion.

By my eighteenth birthday, I had started my love affair with heroin, and this lasted for the next decade. The introduction came via friends in my neighbourhood and very soon I was doing anything I could to get more. Social using or sharing were not in my vocabulary, so I acquired the necessary paraphernalia and locked myself in the bathroom, determined to master the art of self-injecting. I got addicted straight away and the only problem was a financial one.

After a second bout of hepatitis landed me in hospital, I went on a mission to get high as often as possible. I loved the effects of heroin on my being and wanted oblivion, going to any lengths to get it. But my stay at the Tropical & Contagious Diseases department had given away my secret, although by then I had no fear about being exposed. The world did not end, and my parents did not disown me. In all our naivety we cried and hugged, in the belief that the solution was ours to embrace and resolve.

After a liver biopsy and short stay to detox, I left hospital and was back with a vengeance, with no desire to slow down or change. As my secret was now out of the bag, I could dedicate my entire life to my desired drug-induced comatose state. By now my Public Relations & Publicity degree was an inconvenience and failure the only outcome.

My days were consumed with getting and staying high. My future was not part of the equation and heroin addiction was my glamorised, craved reality. My parents continued with their 'saving Alice' project, consisting of stays at the local Drug Dependency Unit, our beach house and hotels to do detoxes, moves to other cities and sessions with psychiatrists who offered counselling and prescribed drugs, including Naltrexone used in the management of alcohol and opiate dependence. My father was told to make me swallow the pill in front of him every day, and as a result my heroin consumption got swapped for lots of cocaine laced with all kinds of alcoholic beverages, as well as other drugs. Swapping and changing became my new way of life for a while.

Eventually we were told about the Narcotics Anonymous (NA) and Familes Anonymous (FA) 12-Steps of Recovery fellowships. My parents grabbed them like life jackets on rough seas. Me? I only wanted to keep using and being happy. I got bribed with cigarettes and was given small change to put in the collection pot used to pay the rent and for coffee. I was driven to meeting room doors most nights, but the inevitable failure of such dedicated efforts by my parents was written in the cards and became apparent early on. For them, though, FA became the answer to all their prayers and soon they were told about 12-Step residential treatment centres in England.

Borrowing money from my granddad was the first move, the second was my dad getting on a plane with me and going to Weston-super-Mare in order to entrust me to the care of strangers who were going to help him save my life. I was twenty-three years old; the rest is, as they say, history.

For me this was indirectly the beginning of my recovery and the rest of my life's journey that forever and very profoundly changed me. I would love to say that from then onwards was all roses, but it was roses riddled with thorns. Staying in a tough, confrontational environment was not for me and the only benefit was a respite from using, which led to a clearer mind and made me think the problem had been sorted as I had abstained for three months.

Homesick and unhappy with the fact that the people in that place seemed to want to keep me there forever as well as change me, I left. To celebrate leaving I drank lager at the airport. My arrival in Lisbon in the middle of summer reinforced a false sense of security and straight after my best friend's wedding that weekend I was back to my old habits.

The year following consisted of more geographical moves and self-imposed detoxes aimed at getting my parents' trust back, but nothing worked. One day at an NA convention in Porto, I met a man, Luis, who I thought would be my saviour. I followed him to England in the hope that a new man and country would be the solution to all my problems. But instead, now I was living and using in London, trying hard to exorcise old demons and come to terms with a termination I'd had before leaving Portugal, which had left me heartbroken.

My problems were compounded when I received an HIV positive diagnosis on top of the hepatitis C, and this was a major factor in most of the decisions I took afterwards. I married Luis and stood by his bedside and watched him die from AIDS, after which using with a vengeance until I died became my mission. By then I believed my diagnosis was a punishment from God for my sins, and I just wanted to wipe out my miserable existence.

When he died in 1993, I recommitted myself to self-destruct by committing crimes and prostituting myself. But, eventually, this soul-destroying lifestyle, combined with a terror of dying alone, brought me to my senses. Finding the meaning of life became my goal; *so, I had to get clean!*

Checking into rehab again was the beginning of a journey of self-discovery, coated with endless emotions and many new relationships. The struggles have been similar to those I've encountered throughout my life, but I now face them rather than run away. Once again, a clear mind was helpful, but the difference was that this time it had been *my* decision to want to live to do stuff and to be happy! It has been an eye-opener, an ongoing path full of tribulations, exciting as well as terrifying along the way.

When I left treatment, I was in love and in lust with Steve, a man who became my partner and ultimately the father of my daughter, Rita.

But being drug-free, in love, and enjoying life does not last forever unless you work hard at them. Being a natural procrastinator, lazy and habitual thrill-seeker isn't helpful, so soon there was trouble in paradise. Abstinence was a must, but everything else was optional, so I opted out of some of NA's suggestions for a healthy recovery. Forget about finding out 'who you really are' because you might be intrinsically bad and mad! I was told to get a sponsor, but didn't want another mother, so I sponsored myself. Consequently, I relapsed twice, because that's what happens when you're not recovering.

Steve and I stayed together for the next fourteen years, but what I thought would be a happy after ending did not happen; neither of us was strong enough to make it last. Pregnancy, pre-eclampsia and a very premature birth almost killed us. Undiagnosed post-natal depression, followed by a year of hep C treatment, was another nail in the coffin, and by the end of it I was ready for the respite that came with smoking copious amounts of skunk.

Rita spent her early months being looked after by nurses at the special care baby unit. This meant bonding did not occur; she was mine, but I did not feel it. I was clueless. I could not understand why I was not a natural-born mother. Slowly but surely things changed, and over the next few years we became joined at the hip and finally she stopped calling me Alice and started calling me Mum. But we never functioned as a family unit and as Rita and I got closer, my relationship with Steve fizzled into insignificance.

Just before my sixth year of being clean, I realised that I had survived a couple of years without the NA fellowship, and this emphasised my belief that my addiction troubles were truly over. However, at the time my anti-retroviral meds were keeping me from eating and sleeping properly, so I started smoking skunk, as Steve was growing and harvesting plants in our home. What started with a couple of joints at night turned into me diving back into addiction and, once again, I was in trouble.

I spent the next four years like a zombie, gravitating towards the drugs and neglecting Rita, the most important person in my life. I plummeted into the depths of despair and isolation and after that the only way was up, or death.

Recommitting to a desired reality and engaging with NA was a God-and-Alice-send. Recovery this time came first, foremost and everything. I got the sponsor I had always denied myself and embraced all the NA fellowship had to offer. I realised I literally knew nothing and finding out that my thought processes were warped and my previous beliefs useless was surprising. A new reality was formed on the basis that the old one was null and void. So began a new existence based on the absence of self. Everything I did had to be shared and checked with another NA member because I did not trust myself any longer.

I have discovered that regular attendance at meetings means a restoration to sanity, a feeling of belonging, an assurance that I am not alone and gives me the therapeutic value of identification. When I serve, I bond; I feel confident and empowered. I learned new skills, practised commitment and responsibility. I am reliable and trustworthy. This fellowship works because I, like every other member, do my bit. I have found a new home where I have a place, and everyone knows me. I am acknowledged, supported and accepted. I have lost most of my fears of being judged, rejected, or abandoned, and practise wholeheartedly being honest, compassionate and real with others. I am taking risks and doing it differently. I am present, alive and still kicking.

The 12-Steps of the NA programme did all this for me and they take my breath away. They may be hard to follow and practise at times, but they are essential and have phenomenal results. The good news is that they are personal; the bad news is that they're an alien concept to most people, but as I was told, 'there is no growth without pain'! Surrendering to the fact that I am an addict in trouble and cannot do it on my own was difficult. Letting go of my will, uncovering and exposing myself, sharing, changing, peeling layers off, constructing a new better self, were difficult but all worth it.

As I got to the written step of making a fearless and thorough moral inventory of myself, procrastination kicked in because it felt as if I had already been enduring this unbearably painful process for a very long time. There were too many overwhelming feelings, too often for my taste, but I saw this process was working for others, so I soldiered on. This is a self-loving, affirming spiritual exercise and today I'm reaping the benefits. Enjoyment has replaced endurance. I'm learning to be gentle with myself and bond with others. Life's still an uncharted territory, but I'm getting ready. I feel older, wiser and more mature. I have found in NA an instruction manual to use till the day I die; and it is a comforting, soothing thought to know that I'll find myself in the process. I can be myself, fully present, and forgive the powers that be in Portugal for the way in which they used to absolve themselves of any responsibility with regards to addicts. But now, Portugal and I have come full circle. My country has become the poster child for a change in attitudes and drug legislation that has hugely transformed the picture.

When I left in 1991, I had already contracted hepatitis C and HIV, as had most of my using acquaintances. There were no needle exchange schemes and pharmacies would refuse to sell syringes to drug users. At out-of-hours chemists the price of injecting equipment would be the same as a wrap of cocaine or heroin. As a result, recycling, sharing, washing, and sharpening were common and contaminated a whole generation. When I arrived in London I was dumbfounded by the endless supply of syringes, tourniquets, sterile wipes and water, disposable bins, etc. The difference was immense.

In 1997 about 45% of reported AIDS cases in Portugal were among intravenous users. By 1999 nearly 1% of the Portuguese population was addicted to heroin and drug-related AIDS deaths were the highest in the European Union.

In the year 2000 the decriminalisation of drugs was being discussed in Portugal's parliament and a year later the policy was changed. As a direct consequence blood-borne, sexually transmitted diseases and drug overdoses have dramatically decreased. Targeting drug use became an effective HIV-prevention measure. My country decided to treat the possession and use of drugs as a public health issue, so instead of a criminal record and/or a prison sentence, addicts would get a fine and/or a referral (that wasn't compulsory) to a treatment programme. As a result, money saved from taking individuals through the criminal justice system started being spent on rehabilitation and get-back-to-work schemes.

In the last fourteen years, drug use has diminished among the fifteen to twenty-four age group. There has also been a decline in the percentage of the population who have ever used a drug and then continued to do so. Drug-induced deaths decreased steeply and at present Portugal has three overdoses per million citizens, compared to the EU average of 17.3. HIV infection has steadily reduced and has become a more manageable problem. There's been a similar downward trend for cases of hepatitis B and C. This policy was complemented by allocating resources to the drugs field, expanding and improving prevention, treatment, harm reduction and social reintegration.

Overall, I wouldn't change my life or regret any part of the journey. It made me who I am – someone determined to make a difference and leave behind a worthwhile legacy. I am also a good daughter, mother to my daughter and partner in the best relationship with a man I ever had.

Chapter 15

Bill's Story – An Indian Connection

My name is Bill M, and I am an alcoholic. I was born in Goa at my grandparents' home and grew up in a middle-class family – Mom, Dad and a younger sister – in Ahmedabad, India. There I went to school and tried my hand at college but dropped out after two years.

I do not know why, but it always felt like I was born under a bad sign (or something!) as 'luck' did not seem to favour me right from the time I began to crawl. 'Bad luck' and 'trouble' seemed to be my only friends. In fact, if it was not for bad luck, I would have had no luck at all!

My father left us when I was four. The feelings of insecurity and inferiority I felt in school and college made me boisterous and rebellious, at times even with the priests and the church, although my maternal family was very religious and pious.

I had a good voice and later became a lead singer with a rock band. I fell in love with a girl, but it took eight years to convince her parents to let us date. I started to climb the ladder of success in my career, attending social gatherings and whoopee parties. At these, aged twenty-two, I was introduced to liquor. My drinking progressed rapidly, as did my music career. But the feeling that I had ARRIVED, in a few short years was replaced by a sense of bewilderment and despair.

I got married when my wife and I were both twenty-six years old. Six years later we were blessed with a son, Raul, who was born with congenital heart disease and at fifteen months had open-heart surgery; the success of both I celebrated with alcohol in the hospital.

Raul grew up without much help or attention from me. Regardless, he excelled both academically and in the sports arena. He went on to become the fastest National In-Line Skater and champion of India. Not only that, he represented our country in the World Championships four times – in France, Italy, Venezuela and Belgium. All through this, I was present, but he hated me for humiliating and disgracing him with my drunken behaviour at these events.

On one such occasion when he was to receive the championship award, I was driving to the venue in my car at breakneck speed when I rammed into a student's vehicle near the university. I was accosted by students on all sides who pinned me down on the road. It was only after a lot of pleading that they let me carry on just to attend my son's award ceremony, but not before giving me a good blasting about drunken driving and my physical condition. If only they had known that I was carrying a bottle to celebrate the occasion! On reaching the skating rink, I made a scene and my wife and son left in disgust. I was doubly miserable as my car, as well as my shattered ego, was also in a sorry state.

At home my disease progressed steadily. All too frequently Raul watched the violent scraps I had with his mother. I often broke crockery in fits of drunken rage and sold household goods to buy alcohol. My friends deserted me, and relatives dared not say the words 'don't drink' to me. I hardly remember how I reached home most evenings, where I had been, who my companions were, and whether I had eaten or not: most often it was well after midnight. At such times I would find out later I had often promised to help out friends, but could not recollect what it was I had to do. The next day, when reminded, I would lie and try and cover up by saying I had been busy and asked them to relate to me again what had to be done.

As a young man I had learned that my father had been an alcoholic and died due to this disease: there and then I had made up my mind not to touch alcohol, but by now it seemed history was about to repeat itself.

Because of my alcoholic drinking I lost my job of 26 years as a junior manager with a reputable company, but we continued to live in a reasonably good apartment block. I managed to get myself elected chairman of this housing block's association. However, soon after they made it clear they distrusted me. By now I was getting desperate; death seemed likely from drinking neat illegal liquor. Thoughts of taking poison or jumping in front of a fast-running train crossed my mind. I was then 51 years of age and 35 kilos in weight.

My wife took a job with a speciality hospital and soon after lovingly pleaded with me to visit the psychiatrist there. I declined, feeling certain this would not help. By now I was beyond trusting anyone or anything.

My son on several occasions begged his mother to leave me and start a fresh life by themselves. At this time, he wrote a letter to me, and although my wife kept telling me to read it, I did not and left it on top of the refrigerator.

On 21st May 2005, an article in the daily newspaper, *Times of India*, headed 'KICK THAT BOTTLE' caught my wife's eye. She flung the newspaper at me and told me to read and act on it before she got back home.

I drank that morning, but by evening the thought of my wife's threat made me frantically search for the newspaper. I read the article which mentioned Alcoholics Anonymous and at the bottom there was a helpline number. I called and in a pathetic lament cried out, 'I am an alcoholic... do you have a solution?' The person on the other end listened to my woes patiently and asked if I could make it to a meeting on Sunday. I did so, travelling 125 km to my very first AA Meeting in Baroda. There were fifteen men at the meeting who were polite and welcomed me; as I listened to them, I tried to hold on to every word they uttered.

The meeting began with the Serenity Prayer followed by several AA readings; its 'Preamble', 'How it works', the '12-Steps', '12 Traditions', '12 Promises', and so on. Some of the men then shared their stories with which I immediately identified. At the end I loved the warmth of the hugs I received as they mentioned that I was not alone in my struggle any more.

The return journey gave me ample time to ponder over the meeting. Phrases like 'Rarely have we seen a person fail who has thoroughly followed our path', 'Keep Coming Back', and 'It Works if You Work It' kept ringing in my ears.

From that day on, I attended meetings every Sunday and Wednesday in Baroda, which was an eight-hour commute with the meeting time. At the end of three months of this, they helped me start a meeting in my home town, Ahmedabad, Gujarat. Every Sunday and Thursday I would open the classroom where the meeting was held and, on many occasions, it would be just me and the God of my understanding who attended.

Gradually we grew in numbers, but I continued my trip to Baroda once a week, thereby making three meetings weekly. Often, I could hardly afford these trips, but I knew that to stay sober I had to make them. On one such visit somebody handed me copies of the books *Alcoholics Anonymous*, *Living Sober*, *Daily Reflections*, *As Bill Sees It*, and all the AA pamphlets, which helped me a lot.

After three months abstinence I plucked up the courage to read my son's letter. Its contents moved me in a way I find hard to express; the words and feelings they provoked were immediately like a prayer to me. It was as though an act of providence had worked through him and brought about the dramatic change in me. I later understood this to be a spiritual awakening, one sufficiently powerful to help bring about my recovery from alcoholism.

This was his prayer to me.

Don't you ever want me to sit next to you and talk to you? Don't you ever want me to respect you as my father? Don't you ever want me to appreciate what you do for us?

Do you think I hate you...? NO, I DON'T... But I do hate the person you become after you drink. Yes, I do hate you like THIS!! Not that I like saying that, I just don't like to see you that way.

I can't hate you; you are my father and maybe I don't say it, but I love you. And maybe you don't say it, but I know you love me too.

It is 2 a.m. and am I writing this letter to ask you WHY...?

It does not mean you stop for a day or two and everything will be fine. It will take time. Don't do it for me, do it for yourself. Try to keep what you have.

Thanks for reading this letter.

Raul

Even when I read it today, nearly fifteen years after he wrote it, the same emotions I had when I first read it in August 2005 bring tears to my eyes.

As time passed, I got involved in AA service, an essential part of recovery from alcoholism. We held community awareness programmes, made visits to hospitals, psychiatrists, and when invited to do so, to the homes of practising alcoholics. Many since have found us and we are now more than fifty members in the three groups.

Though I have remained sober, for some time not much changed in other respects towards my family, friends or society. This situation I shared at meetings and old timers said I should, 'stick with the winners' and 'get a sponsor'. After reading the AA Sponsorship pamphlet, I was ready to get a sponsor and prepared myself by reading about the steps. It was now my luck changed.

At my first AA convention, shortly after I arrived, I was introduced to a very kind man I took an immediate attraction to. As a result, I asked him to be my sponsor and guide me through the AA recovery programme. He gave me a daily regimen to stick to which I found has brought about a total transformation in me. This was to say morning and evening prayers, ring him every day, call at least two other AA members, and read seven to eight pages of the book *Alcoholics Anonymous* in sequence.

This eventually resulted in my coming to believe in a Higher Power. It was significant that AA had to change my focus from 'self' and develop an opposite theme if I was to maintain this miracle. Fortunately, sobriety, service for others and action on the 12-Steps started to cause some change in my soul that gave birth to a new me. I learnt the meaning of what it takes to give unconditional love, just as I had previously been given it.

Life for me changed. Miracles happened one after another in my personal life. My business grew, we moved into a better and more palatial home, uniting with the older members of our families. Now four generations were living under one roof! But I soon came to understand and believe that my material success could not take precedence over my spiritual well-being. I fervently started reaching out to newer areas to work with suffering alcoholics. This included tribal areas and people with special needs.

At this stage I was five years sober and a senior AA member pointed out the importance of the Three Legacies of AA – Recovery, Unity, and Service. I was proposed and elected as a delegate to represent my area at the AA General Service Office for India. My focus turned to work for AA on a national platform carrying the message of hope and recovery to places where it had not yet reached. These included Jabua District in the state of Madhya Pradesh (Central India), Saurashtra and Kutch District of Gujarat State and Shillong in the North Eastern State of Meghalaya.

My horizon in AA has been immensely increased and I am presently applying my efforts to the putting on of conventions, workshops, public information activities, also meeting the press, local government and NGOs, hospitals, educational institutions (University of Social Studies) and so on across the length and breadth of my country.

I came to know the meaning of the AA Responsibility Pledge: 'I am responsible when anyone, anywhere, reaches out for help. I want the hand of AA always to be there; and for that I am responsible', and made myself available. This gets me out of my selfishness and self-centredness, which had been the root cause of all my problems.

Whenever I take a pleasure or business trip out of town, I make it a point to get in touch with the Fellowship of AA there and go to meetings to strengthen my sobriety, even if it is in a language I do not know, fully aware that those there also speak the language of the heart.

I have recently been fortunate to attend the International World Convention at Atlanta, in the USA. The theme was 'Happy, Joyous and Free', which has come true in my life by living this AA programme which is a design for living that works under any conditions.

Although I am still poor at some of it, I find the 'Joy of Living' increases as I study and learn 'The Truth of GOD' and try my best each day to do His will. Even here, right through my thirty days of touring America after the convention, I made meetings at every stop, having connected with them before leaving India. I also visited Akron where AA began in 1935 and the General Service Office in New York from where AA's programme has been delivered to the world for almost eighty years; it was like visiting Bethlehem for a Christian, Jerusalem for a or Jew, Mecca for a Muslim, Banaras for a Hindu or Bodhgaya for a Buddhist: for an alcoholic like me this was Heaven on Earth.

No more do I say I was born under a bad sign. I happily proclaim I am a very lucky man thanks to AA. My luck changed; the stars shine brightly now!

I am reminded of Dr Bob, one of AA's founder's words, which echo my relationship with AA and why I love doing what I do.

1. It is a sense of duty.
2. It is a pleasure.
3. Because in so doing I am paying my debt to the man who took time to pass it on to me.
4. Because every time I do it, I take out a little more insurance for myself against a possible slip.

Chapter 16

Tariq's Story – A Palestinian Connection

My name is Tariq. I am a 50-year-old Palestinian Muslim Arab, married and a father to three beautiful boys. I am also a grateful recovering drug addict and alcoholic.

I got clean and sober on December 22 2006 after waking up in the detox unit of a very fancy and expensive treatment centre in America, yet again, after suffering a massive grand-mal-like seizure from the toxic levels of drugs and alcohol in my body. This was the third time this had happened to me in a few short years, where I ended up in a hospital intensive care unit. Sadly, somehow, I had a few more lessons to learn before I surrendered to the fact that I had a life-threatening problem that had no known cure. My mindset from the beginning, as with that of my family, was that our vast wealth, education and connections would buy me the best medical care and counselling to help cure me of my problem with drinking and prescription drug addiction. It never worked, and I kept inching closer to death every time, until I dove into Alcoholics Anonymous and its sister Narcotics Anonymous after leaving treatment in early 2007.

I was born in Jerusalem and grew up in a loving and supportive family. We lived in many places, as my dad was finishing his graduate studies at Columbia University in New York City and launched a successful career helping develop the infrastructure of a few oil-rich Arab States in the Middle East in the 1970s. We lived in Beirut but travelled around the Middle East a lot. We spent summers in many different parts of it, because of my father's rapidly growing business. Civil War broke out in Lebanon in 1975, but we were lucky to be able to move to Paris in 1976, where my father had many business relationships. It was there the following year, at the age of 13, where I had my first encounter with alcohol and prescription drugs.

My first drinking experience ended up being a blackout, where I consumed enough beer that I could not remember many things about the night, let alone how I got home. My first prescription drug experience was a few months later around an operation I had to undergo for a broken bone fragment I had in my hip/femur socket from playing football. Both experiences with alcohol and the opiate painkillers gave me a tremendous sense of relief and a high that made me feel like I was fearless. For a boy who was cripplingly shy, very self-conscious and suffering from overwhelming low-self-esteem, this was a huge freedom and gave me the joy I was always looking for.

I had finally found a way to function and thrive in a world that I felt I did not fit into. I seemed to be developing a survival skill to overcome my problems coping with life as I experienced it. Exaggerating things, lying and taking off into a world of fantasy in my mind were some of the ways I coped with my awkwardness. I even surprised my mother with one of these coping skills when we met the principal of the school my parents had applied to send me to.

I was asked by him what my name was. I whispered that my name was Tariq, panicking that he might reject me because I was dark-skinned and had an alien name for an American school. He confirmed my worst fears by asking me to say my name twice and then having me spell it out loud for him. I was horrified. He then asked me if I had an easier to pronounce nickname, at which I quickly said, 'Yes!' My mother looked curiously at me waiting to hear what was going to come out of my mouth… I said loudly, 'You can call me Ronnie!' My mother had the most puzzled look on her face, but said nothing to avoid embarrassing me. From that point on, in all my schools and universities I was known as Ronnie!

I did not do any more drugs until I was eighteen, but my drinking took hold of me gradually and steadily, and as a result, I became a weekend binge drinker in High School.

We moved to London from Paris in 1978. I was good at athletics, and sports were also my way of fitting into my ever-changing surroundings. Every time I went out drinking with my rugby teammates or other friends from my school or when I was on holiday with other young peers, I would be the one challenging everyone to see how much more we could drink while still being functional. I had incredible endurance with drinking by the time I was eighteen and a deepening relationship with the escape and relief that alcohol brought.

I was good enough at running/athletics that I was offered a scholarship to attend a prominent university in Texas. I was incredibly proud of this, as my academic performance in school were Bs and Cs (gentleman's grades, I told my parents!) but not the exceptional academic levels that my older brother got, or top marks my father had achieved, and been awarded academic scholarships for, which was how he overcame the poverty of being a Palestinian refugee.

So I saw this athletic scholarship opportunity as my destiny, to do something my dad would be proud of and to become independent early on in my young adult life.

I got to Texas, and boy did they do everything big! Drinking was a varsity sport and I really took to it. I also got into smoking marijuana, tried acid (LSD), free-based cocaine, and snorted it – all in my first year. Within the same year, because of all these distractions, I got kicked off the Track Team and eventually got kicked out of the university, because I simply did not show up. The lies, the anxiety and pain of losing my newfound independence and potential grew agonisingly intense, but I medicated those feelings away with drugs and alcohol. The incredible disappointment of my parents was very painful to bear, too, but I was permanently sufficiently medicated not to let it bother me too much anymore.

I woke in up in Washington, DC in August of 1983 at the age of 19 with a brand-new opportunity to start again. My dad got me into a new university, got me a grand apartment, and a new car. My dad and my brother were great at trying to fix things for me and clearing up the wreckage I would leave behind. Within one year of being in Washington, I had surrounded myself with friends in the nightclub life. I also managed to join a tough city gym that many policemen worked out in. Everybody in the early 1980s was taking steroids, and I joined in, a short cut of sorts to being super-strong and fit. We would go to the manager's office in the back, pay for it, drop our shorts, and get the shots in our thigh muscles. I started squatting and bench-pressing weights beyond my ability and ended up rupturing two discs in my lower back. Soon after, I returned to London, where my parents had remained since leaving Lebanon, to have a serious operation to remove the ruptured discs.

The operation involved opening me up from the front and the back, including taking a bone graft from my hip to put in place of the ruptured discs. It was painful, and the post-op recovery was long and slow. I was in a private hospital on Harley Street, London for nearly a month. Opiate painkillers became my new best friend. I remember I used to argue and fight with the nurse and matron that I needed another morphine shot because the pain was so bad an hour or two after the previous shot was administered. Normally they are meant to last for 4-6 hours. I had a voracious appetite for these anesthetics, just like I had for alcohol. I loved the way the made me feel – as if I had no cares in the world at all and not having to feel any of the building remorse I had about all my missed opportunities.

After losing a complete semester of university I returned to continue my undergraduate education. My drinking took off again, but now I had an additional fixation on the opiate painkillers and other pills in the benzodiazepine family, like Valium or Xanax. The people I got to know and spend time with, and money on, grew darker. I still managed to finish my undergraduate education, but it took an extra year with my back operation and failing a few courses along the way. It was a mess. I always had the best intentions, a lot of ambition, a kind and generous heart, but something always got in the way of that translating into my reality.

In 1987 my father created a new opportunity for me to get some work experience at Morgan Stanley in New York City, and take some courses at his alma mater, The Graduate School of Business at Columbia University. He lavished me with a gorgeous apartment overlooking the Hudson River on the Upper West Side on Riverside Drive, and I was all set to realise a lot of personal growth and opportunities ahead. The mixture of pills and alcohol began to affect my moods, and my ability to show up and function. Even with a long-time girlfriend, I had trouble showing up consistently and even sexually. I remember becoming depressed and suicidal at one point, despite all the opportunities and second chances I was given. I just could not understand what was wrong with me. I knew I was intelligent, kind and full of energy, but why was I feeling the opposite of all of that?

I bailed out of New York, Morgan Stanley, Columbia University and the beautiful apartment after only one year. It was a bad experience that would leave a very bitter sense of myself and my abilities. I went back to Washington, DC where my dad had bought a big house with a swimming pool and loads of entertainment space for my brother and me. (I later found out he did that to keep me under my brother's watchful eye, as my downward spiral was becoming more and more obvious.)

I was now 24 years old and working with my brother at a very cool company he had started a short time after earning his Juris Doctorate in Law and his MBA with honours from Georgetown University. I managed to function, but I was not consistent. My focus was on the party scene, girls and travelling. I had become increasingly unreliable.

In the period from 1988 to 1994, I was searching and trying to hold on to what felt like a sacred calling to find a way to live up to all my aspirations and dreams, but my connection with myself and to the world was disintegrating. I tried spiritual workshops and healing programmes, including Life Spring, an offshoot of EST, which was about finding one's self, and also kind of cultish. I always felt amazing for some time after completing the various levels of these programmes, but soon after I would begin to sink into the same old pattern of materialism, self-indulgence, instant gratification and escapism. My dad gave me a book called *The Road Less Travelled*, by M Scott Peck, but I could not get into it, even though I had it by my bedside along with other personal growth and spiritual books. I had found out this world best-selling book had a chapter on 'delayed gratification'; it was no wonder I could not get into it!

My parents were determined to help me settle down. My mother made a suggestion that I meet a beautiful 22-year-old Palestinian Muslim woman who was the daughter of one of her relatives in Jerusalem. She had been educated in the West, and was very kind and gorgeous. I figured I could make my parents happy, marry the woman of their dreams, and get material rewards and some peace of mind from my increasingly troubled, hollow life.

I pursued her, charmed her and disarmed her with my amorous advances and proposed to her. My father was so pleased that he spent several million pounds on a huge wedding at the Park Lane Hotel in London, in 1995. He then went further and bought us a brand-new gorgeous grand house in Washington, DC.

After two years settling into married life in our beautiful home, with our two cars, and the big bank account my father lavished me with, things were getting worse. I started bribing pharmacists to give me opiate painkillers and sedatives. I was drinking nearly every evening – and I blamed it on having a tough time adjusting to my wife and married life. I felt more and more lonely, despite having an amazing woman by my side, travelling around the world, and every material comfort.

I started having problems with my health. I got shingles, which was painful, so the doctor gave me opiate painkillers. I had dental surgery on my gums, and got more narcotic opiates. As I was neglecting my back, and not doing the maintenance to keep it in good shape, which resulted in lower back pain, so other doctors gave me narcotic painkillers and strong muscle relaxants. Not once did any of them mention the dangers of the habit-forming nature of these pills, and I did not resist the generous quantities being prescribed, as I was loving them. When I had psoriasis breaking out on my skin, not knowing that was from the increasingly toxic levels of opiates in my system, I managed to get more opiates out of the specialists who saw me for the rash. I had a deviated septum in my nose, so I jumped at the opportunity to have a very painful operation, just so I could get more opiates, and sedatives too!

Not long after, I had a massive falling out with my brother at work. I decided I had had enough of Washington, DC and convinced my wife to move to Toronto. My addiction and drinking really took off there, as I had loads of extra money from the sale of my house and a gorgeous two-level penthouse in Yorkville, the best shopping and bar district in Toronto. I quickly found that prescription laws in Canada for opiates and sedatives were more relaxed than in the US. I made friends with two neighborhood pharmacists, and started getting opiates and sedatives from them. Sometimes I would get prescriptions from our local doctor to cover the pharmacist's exposure. I then started to give gifts to my doctor, in return for more prescriptions. Eventually I bought him a brand-new car!

Many times, along the way, I realised that I was in the grip of something that was beginning to scare me and isolate me from myself, and my life. I tried so many times to taper down the doses slowly and manage my own withdrawal, but whenever I got close to getting off completely or was very close, I found that I could not cope with life and my feelings, and went right back into drugs; and every time I was sinking deeper into addiction.

Mixing alcohol with this mixture of drugs gave me nightmares when I was awake. I would try to sleep, when suddenly I would fly out of bed, as I felt my breathing had stopped or was very close to it. But did I stop as a result, no… that was the insanity of what was happening to me, yet I was not conscious my behaviour was so insane.

In the next few years, I became fully addicted to opiates and sedatives. I was taking up to 100 Percocet (an opiate painkiller, that was 5 mg of Oxycodone and 325mg of Acetaminophen – opiate and Tylenol Paracetamol). By then I was in all kinds of pain, including the feeling of being more alone than ever, despite having two beautiful children and my wife around me. I spent more and more time alone in my bed in our penthouse, isolating myself, making excuses not to go out and be with people, including my own family. I even made up a huge lie, that I had cancer, in order to justify why I was losing weight, looking awful and isolating so much. All my friends, my wife and family believed me, as why else would I be so ill all the time and look the way I did?

Soon after I started telling this story, I had great difficulty breathing and pain in my sides. I had lost a lot of weight, as I would starve myself to get more effect from the opiates, plus it helped me avoid being constipated from them.

That in turn made me vomit and feel nauseous. My weight had come down to 68 kg from 88 kg when I got married eight years before.

One very bad night, my wife took me to the emergency department at Mount Sinai hospital. I had no idea why I felt so ill, but it turned out that my liver was failing and both lungs were filling with fluid. I was moved to intensive care for a few days and put on a ventilator. I remember even conning the intensive care nurse into giving me more morphine and he obliged. I was so out of my mind and my body was numb. When I had to fess up with the truth of what I was doing to myself and confess to my wife that I was not ill with cancer and admit the vast quantities of drugs that I was consuming, the doctors at Mount Sinai said it was impossible that I could have lived and survived while consuming such large quantities. I learned that apart from the obvious danger of the opiates stopping my breathing, which had begun to happen, the Acetaminophen (Tylenol or Paracetamol/Panadol) nearly killed my liver. The alcohol, of course, was helping to push my liver over the edge.

My brother and father flew to Toronto as my situation was critical and decided to fly me by private jet to the Cleveland Clinic in Ohio to get more intensive care and a detox. After a couple of weeks there, it seemed my body had survived its near-death experience, and I was checked into its addictions treatment. As soon as I arrived, even though I was only on a low dose of opiates for discomfort and pain, I was immediately put on a high dose of methadone, another opiate, which gave me an amazing high. This, they told me, was the beginning of a methadone detox, where they would taper the dose quickly over ten days. The come-down and withdrawals from the methadone were more vicious than anything I had ever experienced.

The Cleveland Clinic used the 12-Step programmes of Alcoholics Anonymous and Narcotics Anonymous. I used to go their meetings and think what a sorry bunch of people they were. The medical director of the treatment centre told me that I would have to go into long-term care to sort out my issues, start attending daily meetings of AA and NA, and live with these two spiritual programmes for the rest of my life. I recoiled, as I had this vision of living a spiritual, sober and clean life being like a castrated monk living in a tower all alone with no joy, fun or passion – conveniently forgetting that the drugs and the alcohol had reduced me to that, although I was far from being a monk! I was also terrified if I delved into all of my issues and opened the door to the troubles deep inside me, I would not know what I would find. I had lost most of my true identity and was afraid of who or what was left without the drugs and alcohol that had held me together. So I hired a private jet and escaped back to Toronto in the middle of the night.

I moved my family to London a year later hoping that would fix me. My wife was pregnant with son number three, so I was going to be helpful to her and my parents and put the messy past in North America behind me. I found the stress of being around my mother, who had advanced Alzheimer's disease, and my father, who had cancer, very difficult and heart-breaking. My new home, child on the way, new schools, etc. all overwhelmed me. So in order to cope, I started having the occasional drink, but to my surprise I found that getting narcotic painkillers (DF 118s) from the local pharmacist without a prescription was very easy in the UK. I also began taking lots of sedatives as well, which I could also get without a prescription from our friendly local pharmacist. Needless to say, I got hooked again and the quantities I took rose quickly. I was soon taking over forty DF 118s and three to four 5 mg Xanax a day. I had started sourcing my supply from a few friendly doctors, but I also started paying 'gifts' in cash to my area pharmacist. On December the 16th that year, I ended up having my third seizure, right in front of my dad and brother and just minutes after dropping the kids off to school. I was ambulanced and hospitalised again.

A few days later I woke up at a treatment facility in America in a detox ward next to a guy who was sobbing non-stop when he was awake. I felt the same, but could not cry. It was a very difficult seven weeks that I spent there. The detox they used was Subutex (an opiate antagonist drug used for withdrawals from narcotics) which was very difficult to break away from. I could not sleep for the first four weeks for more than an hour a night. It was horrendous, but I began to see the truth of my situation and had a chance to express my feelings of remorse to men and women who were stricken with the same affliction.

I got home in early February of 2007 and was told to go to meetings to help me stay clean and sober, but I thought I was sorted and was better than ever. It took only two weeks for me to be overwhelmed again and back in my reality completely unanesthetised. I wanted to use drugs and ran to one of my pharmacists to get some, despite my wife and family telling me explicitly if I did go back to my old ways, they would walk away from me. It had to be an act of God, but the pharmacist was ill and not coming in for a few days, so I had no option but to run to the AA meeting that was down the street and confess how desperately difficult it had been coming back to my life and how badly I wanted to use and drink again.

It was at that very first AA meeting in London where I heard the same stories as mine repeated. I had wonderful and very kind people I had never met before coming up to me after and offering me support, hugs and phone numbers to contact them. One particular man took the time and expense to buy me an AA book and offered to guide me and help me. From then on, he became my AA/NA sponsor, a guide of sorts who had been through much the same humiliations I had with drugs, but found a much more powerful and meaningful way to live through the 12-Steps of AA and NA.

My life changed. I found the immense difficulty in assuming my life as a son, brother, husband and father of three boys much easier with the support of my sponsor, the multitude of meetings we had in London, and the service work I volunteered to do among the fellowships of AA and NA. My sense of worth grew as I found out I was not alone in suffering from terrible remorse and shame. I was among a tribe of fellow sufferers whose lives were slowly coming back together. As I followed their examples, the healing process of working these truly spiritual programmes opened the door to a life beyond anything I could have imagined possible, and all the time since my mind has been clear of all mood-altering substances.

The slow process of rebuilding my life with everything around me, including myself, was difficult for the first year or two. My family began to trust me again. My children were not so afraid of me anymore or worried if I would die. I had unforgettable moments when travelling on vacations to places like Nice where I had partied and played for years, but never sober. I was reduced to tears by the beauty of the surroundings that I was never able to appreciate before. My mind was connected to my awakened heart, thanks to AA and NA.

Among the blessings I have received I have come to believe that love is the answer to all the world's problems and the rest is bullshit. When people connect with love, so do their families; and that's what the programmes of AA and NA offer. I believe the world's problems are growing partly because of the disintegration/fragmentation of families; whereas in both our fellowships all around me I see that recovery through love in families is huge. If this could be applied in countries like Palestine and Israel, where my heart lies, a solution to the troubles there would be inevitable.

But the single biggest gift of my recovery so far, apart for being clean and sober for over twelve years, is that I have fallen in love with my wife for the very first time. It reduces me to tears every time I think on just how far away from the abyss AA and NA has brought me from that dark place I once lived. Today I am fully alive and in love with everything, because the 12-Step programmes I practise in my daily life opened the door for me to love and accept myself for the first time. Very simply, fear and emptiness have been replaced by Love and fulfilment.

Chapter 17

Nina's story – A French Connection

I am an alcoholic. But I was not someone who finished up as a tramp, in a mental institution or knocking on death's door, though I almost reached each of these points because my disease led me to a dark place, ending with my living in a permanent state of desperation.

I was born on 25th December 1967, Jesus's birthday, in Tahiti. My parents were French, happy young newlyweds, and in many ways it would seem I had been born in paradise. But because of my underlying mental state I soon became a restless, irritable and discontented person.

Life started to be difficult for me when I was a teenager. I was self-centred and selfish; all I thought about were the awful conditions in my life, never the positives. This meant I was almost permanently depressed, causing me to feel empty, as though I had a hole in both my heart and soul. As a result, at the age of fourteen, I began using cannabis and prescription drugs; the latter I stole from my mother's medicine cabinet. I had started to blame my parents and teachers for how I felt.

By now we had moved to France and I had become aware of my father's background. He was the orphan son of a German soldier, who had been stationed in France in the war, and my French grandmother. This kind of combination, history proves, causes a lack of identity and mental disturbance to their children. In the community, they were not liked and there was much shame, which must have been difficult for their mothers.

I knew my mother was the child of an alcoholic and her father had died as a result. Today I know my parents loved me, but they were dysfunctional, and these conditions contributed indirectly to my drug abuse. I was not beaten or abused, but I still ended up an alcoholic and drug addict. I had a good education, but I did not feel understood or secure and lacked love and attention. My father was strict and authoritarian, and, because of his work, he was absent for considerable periods of time. My mother was always emotionally unstable and very negative.

By the age of sixteen I was having problems with prescription drugs, feeling more and more isolated and lonely even after taking them. On one occasion I had taken the pills and decided to go hitch-hiking by myself, something I had done with friends several times. A man picked me up and sometime later he abused me. I vaguely remember being raped, but mostly I was in blackout. Under the circumstances I buried this event.

From the age of seventeen, for four years I had an alcoholic boyfriend who introduced me to several drugs. But I didn't care about his alcoholism as long as he provided the drugs I needed. I carried on like this for a few years and every substance I took was to help me run away from my head; to stop the noise and critical voices. All I wanted was to be removed from the very dark places that filled my mind and I would do anything I thought would achieve that.

The one highlight in my life was doing a history of art degree at Toulouse University. From there I studied at the Louvre in Paris and both I really enjoyed. The trouble was that when I finished, I had no idea what to do and was frightened of the future; inside I felt empty. I thought life was too difficult and unmanageable.

Ever since my mid-teens men had found me attractive. At twenty-four I met a man, a doctor, and became his girlfriend. I wasn't really fond of him, but he could prescribe me drugs and that was interesting; and that was what he did. These included amphetamines, and very soon I also began to drink heavily to increase the effect of the drugs. I carried on like this for a few months and in doing so my problems mounted. It was then I crossed the bridge from being a drug user to an addict.

I now had two jobs and was living in a Paris flat my parents bought for my sister and me. I did not pay them the rent we agreed as money for drugs was the most important thing in my life. For the same reason I messed up opportunities that would have led me to a good professional life, even though I was ambitious and intelligent. I had good networking opportunities, but could not use them properly because alcohol and drugs had become more important.

I had my first alarm call when I was twenty-seven. I had stopped the amphetamines, but carried on drinking more and more. One night I was in Paris walking in the street drunk when a man became aggressive towards me. Nothing else happened, but next morning I woke up with a terrible hangover and fear from the night before. I saw my sister, who said I had a problem with alcohol and should go to Alcoholics Anonymous. It was not the first time I had heard about AA, but it was the first time I thought it applied to me and the shock and confrontation with reality was so violent that I was very angry with my sister. I was also almost anorexic and had been fired from a job in a luxury department store for stealing clothes.

The combination of these problems caused me to go my first AA meeting. I went full of fear and humiliation. But there everyone was welcoming and kind and I have a good memory of this experience. After that I went to meetings once a week for two months as, at that time, I thought it was enough not to drink. I now know I was not ready to live without alcohol and when I found another job, I thought I had opened a new page of my life.

After a few months being abstinent on my own, I met a man in a bar who was an artist from Morocco. I began using alcohol again and had the illusion I could control my drinking, even though I had heard in AA that being 'powerless over alcohol' is the alcoholic's problem. I did not accept this applied to me, even though I could not stop and frequently ended in blackout.

My new friend promised me a new life and I thought that from now on it would be different. Again, I was not happy in any aspect of my life and, as an artist, he made me his agent, so I thought I had nothing to lose.

He was from Casablanca and married to a French woman in Paris. For seven years we stayed together travelling regularly to Morocco and New York and had what I thought was an exciting bohemian lifestyle, meeting lots of writers and artists and going to lovely places. He was funny, but he was also tough, and we were not really compatible. In retrospect I wasted a lot of time with him and subconsciously I knew this was the case. But because I thought these lifestyle influences should make my life interesting, I could not see the link between this and my obsession with drink, even though I was destroying my life. I now know I was in denial.

Every day at 4 p.m. we began to drink together, and it was like that for a long time. But it became so bad I could not hide it. One day after a drinking party I woke up and, in a desperate state, I remembered AA. I realised I could not go on like this and went to a meeting. That is where my journey out of the abyss began and I have been following this path for more than fifteen years. I have not consumed alcohol or taken addictive drugs since.

My recovery started when I took AA's Step 1; this meant I admitted that I was powerless over alcohol and that my life had become unmanageable. This second time of going to AA I felt completely empty inside. I was unemployable, had a difficult relationship with my parents and sister, had no real friends, only my lover, and my life was miserable. I was like a walking dead person.

So, on 1st March 2004 for the first time I took my alcoholic state and need for abstinence seriously. Today I live a healthy life; in fact, I built a new one. I even stopped smoking, all thanks to my working AA's 12-Steps of recovery programme which has also resulted in my embarking on a spiritual journey.

Previously my sexual relationships had been a disaster, ending in tears and several abortions. I was thirty-six years old but mentally fourteen; I now know I had stopped growing up when I began using mood-altering substances.

Today I have a good job in fine art, a reasonable income, my relations with my parents are good, and most of the time they are with my sister. Achieving this has not always been easy but the programme helps and I am hopeful we can become good friends and like sisters in due course.

I have a new life in London, where I came to live over six years ago to improve my job and English. I am still recovering from the disease of addiction because I know now that alcohol and drugs are not the problem. As we say in AA, 'I came for my drinking but I stay for my thinking.' This is because alcoholism or drug addiction is a mental and emotional illness, also physical and spiritual. In my case I have an allergy to alcohol and drugs. When I took the first glass of wine, beer, whiskey, vodka or other addictive drug I could not stop. So today these obsessions are not in my mind and I am grateful I quit. I am also proud of my sobriety, although life in sobriety has been challenging at times.

For example, I had a problem when I was four years sober. I had met a man who I really liked, and we had stayed together a year. But unbeknown to me he was not always faithful or honest. The result was that in February 2008 I was diagnosed as HIV positive. At the time this made my recovery difficult, but, with the help and support of friends in AA, I got through it and since this experience I have a better comprehension of myself. This was one of the biggest problems I have had in recovery and the 12-Steps helped me deal with it without taking drugs, also to grow mentally and spiritually.

In recent years I have applied the programme more and more in all areas of my life, especially at work where I sometimes found it difficult to cope with people. It has also helped me deal with friends, family and men. By listening to other AA members describe their experiences and identifying with them, and being honest, I have found many similarities, including sometimes the feeling of desperation. The overall result is that I came to believe there is 'something' higher than me that I can call on for help and give me the comfort I need to deal with life on a daily basis. I learned this by getting on my knees and praying.

I was agnostic when I came to the rooms of AA, but I was always searching for something that could help me with my feelings of anxiety, insecurity, anger, loneliness, depression and the dark negative stuff in my head. But as soon as I began to pray to God for a sober day and say thank you on my knees at night for my sober day, my perspective began to change, as did everything in my life. This was just after having that affair and God seemed to know how much I needed help. I now accept I received it from my Higher Power, as we say in AA, but also from the members of the fellowship. I firmly believe I am fortunate to be a member of Alcoholics Anonymous, otherwise I would surely have died, relapsed or gone crazy, especially if I had tried to go through this drama on my own.

One of AA's suggestions is to take an inventory of ourselves. Recently I made one of my defects of character, such as my behaviour, attitudes and negative aspects of my life. This highlighted that the current ones are related to my ego, which convinces me that alcoholism and addiction are more than just drinking or drug abuse problems. It is an invisible enigmatic disease and, because of addicts' natural tendencies towards negative thinking, it does not seem to want them to get well. So, I had to find a framework or structure that would help me cope with life and AA's programme did that.

It started with the principle contained in all religions, that of knowing myself and being true to who I really am. I knew from this inventory that I am a human being and not a monster; I have good and bad within me and I need to be aware of the bad. Once uncovered, it is then possible in Steps six and seven to ask God to remove these challenging aspects of my character such as intolerance, impatience, arrogance, self-pity, resentment and the fear drivers which were at the root of my former mental state. But if I ask for God's help, I live my life knowing my Higher Power will not give me more than I can handle in just one day. Every morning I try to remember this principle and, when I do, I can go forward in the belief that my life will continue to improve.

This applies to my move to London, where sometimes I have had problems with the language and culture. Living here I also find is more expensive than Paris and my job is demanding, but I can cope with all this because I stick to living my life one day at a time and my 'Higher Power is in charge' formula for life.

Today I also meditate, which is suggested in AA's steps. This helped me find, and now maintains, the peace of mind I have found on my spiritual journey. It is an approach I very much appreciate and the best solution to find and maintain peace of mind and happiness. All my life I wanted to feel freedom, and this is one of Alcoholics Anonymous's 12 Promises. As I reflect on them, I am confident the best is yet to come:

We are going to know a new freedom and a new happiness. We will not regret the past nor wish to shut the door on it. We will comprehend the word serenity and we will know peace. No matter how far down the scale we have gone, we will see how our experience can benefit others. That feeling of uselessness and self-pity will disappear. We will lose interest in selfish things and gain interest in our fellows. Self-seeking will slip away. Our whole attitude and outlook upon life will change. Fear of people and of economic insecurity will leave us. We will intuitively know how to handle situations which used to baffle us. We will suddenly realize that God is doing for us what we could not do for ourselves.

Are these extravagant promises? We think not. They are being fulfilled among us—sometimes quickly, sometimes slowly. They will always materialize if we work for them.'

From page 83 of AA's book, *Alcoholics Anonymous*.

Chapter 18

Brian's Al-anon Story

My name is David and I am a grateful member of Al-Anon. I was a professional soldier, happily married with two young daughters. My life was good, my career exciting and rewarding, my family a delight and we had just started a new posting in Edinburgh. Indeed, *life* was good.

"Your wife has cancer," the doctor told me. "She is going to die."

A widower with two children, a career and family life strangely at odds, I was in constant fear of not coping, of losing control, of getting it wrong. Insecure and emotional, I struggled on.

I did cope. I moulded my little one-parent family into an insular threesome, and played up the 'plucky-young-widower-and-his-doting-children' to feed a narcissistic and self-indulgent lifestyle. I presented a picture of a competent and able man making the best of his sad situation. It was an illusion.

Five years on I went to lunch with old friends. The other guest was witty and charming. She had a cigarette in one hand and a glass of wine in the other. I knew she was the one.

I saw her another couple of times before she went home. I rang her up, told her I was about to be posted to Africa, and asked if she'd marry me and come too. She said yes.

I now had two daughters, two stepdaughters, three dogs, a new wife and a new job in a new country.

Life was a ball. Our house was constantly full of visitors, every night seemed to be party night, the whisky flowed and we were everyone's best friends. The girls appeared to flourish, acquaintances and visitors multiplied, and the sun shone.

Our tour finished and we got posted to Aldershot in November. Have you been to Aldershot in November? No sunshine; no staff; no friends, BUT the whisky flowed and we pretended everything was fine.

I took charge. I did the shopping, the cooking, the ironing. I controlled the finances, I dominated the household and I directed the family. I told them what to wear, when and with whom they could go out, how they were to behave. Resentful, angry and confused I shouted, cajoled and pleaded with my family to do it my way so we could all be happy again. It didn't work.

Exhausted, martyred and angry I came home one day to be told by my wife that she had been to an AA meeting and that she was an alcoholic.

An alcoholic? I didn't believe it. But she had a book telling her what to do, a list of meetings that she was encouraged to attend, and a delightful new friend.

I was looking forward to working with this new friend to sort my wife out once and for all. Here was something else for me to take charge over.

The new 'friend' turned out to be an AA sponsor, and she didn't want or need my help. However, she did think my desire to take over my wife's recovery was going to lead to problems, so she suggested I joined AA's sister fellowship, Al-Anon.

I went to Al-Anon meetings and listened to the stories of others whose lives had been affected by alcoholism. I went to open AA meetings to learn about alcoholism. I read literature about this 'family disease'. I attended conventions and asked a long-time member to be my sponsor.

I whinged a lot about my wife and children. I volunteered to be the Group Representative. They thanked me, and made me the tea person! I hung on to the Al-Anon slogans, 'Let go and Let God', but immediately demanded to know why HE hadn't fixed it yet. I took it 'easy' and complained that just made matters worse, and I tried to THINK my way better. But I kept going. I slowly learnt to listen; yes, listen! I realised that I was quite good at being quiet while others spoke, but had no idea how to LISTEN.

My Al-Anon programme gave me the tools to help my spiritual growth, but I tended to use them to metaphorically bludgeon my poor wife while she was struggling to maintain her sobriety. I had read the steps, but was reluctant to look too closely at myself, and I certainly didn't see my shortcomings as such. I was a soldier and surely control and manipulation were just other words for 'leadership' and 'man-management'?

Things reached a crisis at about the three-year point I thought I was doing rather well and that SHE was lagging behind, and not 'recovering' fast enough. I hadn't seen a single amend yet and I reckoned I was owed hundreds!

I decided enough was enough and sat down with my wife to explain why our marriage was over.

Our one remaining dog was very uncomfortable with the atmosphere and made it clear. We decided to take him for a walk to settle him down, and finish our conversation later. At some point on that walk we agreed that the only thing going for us was a mutual belief that we belonged together. On that one belief we determined to hold hands and jump into the unknown and commit ourselves to saving our marriage. The best decision I ever made!

Now I felt the need to REALLY get on with my programme. I found a new sponsor, I did more service, I attended more meetings, read the literature, began to pray and started to work the steps. I stopped looking for a God of other people's understanding and tried to find one of my own. He found me – a loving, amused and omnipresent power that guided my thoughts and deeds. A God that answered my prayers with a yes, or a no or a wait. A God who put situations, people and places in my life to show me things.

We were posted, again, and I started a rather dull deskbound new job in Germany. I had managed Al-Anon's first three steps, but was struggling with the fourth – taking a fearless and moral inventory of myself. But I was busy, and there were other things demanding my attention.

One morning I was told to pack up my desk and move a few miles up the road to take charge of the Joint Services Parachute Centre. Readers with military experience will have witnessed the eccentric internal workings of the MoD. I was a military paratrooper, known to the skydiving community as a 'dope-on-a-rope'. The free-fall school was staffed by experienced free-fall parachutists – graceful sky gods to the likes of me.

There I was, in charge, and totally inexperienced. The staff encouraged me into a student's jumpsuit and went about teaching me to skydive. After a number of jumps they decided I was good enough to go solo. This meant I had to pack my own parachute.

'Why can't he do it?' I asked, pointing at some competent-looking chap. 'Your life depends on it – don't you want to pack it yourself?'

No, was the honest answer. I really didn't want that responsibility.

Once airborne I had to open the door, look down, and drop a paper streamer to assess the wind, then, based on what I'd seen, decide at what point to exit.

'No, no, no – just tell me when to go, and I'll jump.'

'Don't you want to take responsibility for where you land?'

Once again the honest answer was no. I wanted someone else to. Then, they told me, I would free fall from 12,500 feet to 1,500 feet (about 50 seconds) before pulling the rip cord and deploying my 'chute. I now developed huge doubts and was riddled with fears, not of dying, but of getting it wrong, looking stupid, not living up to my self-image. I wanted guarantees, I didn't like taking things on trust. I scrambled into the plane.

At the right height, and at the right point, I jumped. It was magic. The view over the wonderful green North German countryside was spectacular; the curvature of the earth, the wonderful feeling of freedom, speed and exhilaration, and the sheer joy of being suspended in the moment were amazing.

My chute opened and I landed with the style and grace of a gently blown dandelion seed and I knew how much I had learnt that day – not about skydiving, but about me. I saw that I had issues about taking responsibility, that I had to learn what was God's job, and what was mine. I had learnt about the joy of living in and for the moment and about faith, faith in myself and faith in my ability to handle outcomes. I had started my Step Four.

Taking my inventory, talking it through with a trusted friend, and becoming ready to have God remove my shortcomings were liberating experiences. I looked hard at my motives and my actions. I explored my resentments, fears and shame. I came to see that I had grown up in a dysfunctional family and my ability to deal with emotions, with reality and with relationships had been damaged. I prayed for the willingness and courage to change.

I started to take responsibility for myself, to look after my health and well-being. I got my teeth fixed, my damaged knee repaired and rehabilitated. I stopped smoking, got fit again. I gave responsibilities back to those from whom

I'd taken them in the first place, and I allowed my family members to be themselves, to enjoy their own successes, and to cope with their own failures and disappointments. I learnt to love and respect myself and others. In short, I began to mature.

My relationships improved. My wife became my special and equal partner, and we flourished as a couple and a team. We supported each other on our separate recovery journeys and reached a point where we were able to hold our own meetings, just the two of us sharing our experience, strength and hope. We have our own yellow card – Who you see here, What you hear here, When you leave here let it stay here – to ensure our meetings don't follow us to the kitchen sink.

Chapter 19

Neil's Story – A Welsh Connection

I grew up in Swansea, South Wales. When relatives or grown-up friends of my parents came to visit our family in the two-up, two-down (three-down including the extension) terraced house in this industrial city, I was out the door, gone, as fast as I could, but without being impolite. I'd stay for some small talk, agony though it was having to answer such complicated questions as, 'How are you, Neil?'

After I'd been as sociable as my panic-stricken nature would stand I legged it, usually to the banks of the nearby river where I'd take a lonely walk as far as the railway viaduct, past the abandoned copper-smelting works, over the polluted ground where not much grew, happy to be alone and isolated.

I could not stand being around people until, one day, I took five slugs of my parents' whisky and gin. Sometime before this memorable event, I had been saying goodbye to my Auntie Meg at the bus station and noticed someone falling around, slurring his speech. I asked my mother why he was like that and her reply, that he was drunk, intrigued me. The man boarded the bus, sat behind Meg, and vomited on her coat. I don't recall what subsequently happened, but the incident made such an impression as to inspire my ten-year-old self to steal the aforementioned spirits from my mum and dad.

They were both at work. I had the house to myself, so I quickly downed the foul-tasting, burning liquid and waited till the chemical started working.

And it worked very well! I loved the feeling it gave me. Warmth, both physical and mental, flowed through my pre-adolescent body. That was the very beginning of how I viewed any chemical intake, legal or illegal, for the next twenty-seven years. My philosophy on life was formed at the moment whisky and gin had their combined effect on me: drunkenness!

I experimented with other drugs, mostly illegal: cannabis, LSD (this was the late 1960s) Black Bombers, a colloquialism for Durophet, which was prescribed for my mother as an appetite suppressant, Valium, also prescribed to Mum to come down off the Durophet. Amphetamines tend to make people nervous, so, naturally, a doctor, having no knowledge in those days how addictive bombers are, would prescribe Valium, not realising how addictive that substance is too. In other words, my mother in the morning took off like a rocket on speed, then had a very soft landing in the evening with 10 or 20 mgs of Valium. One day I said to her, 'Do you realise how addictive these things are?' She looked at me quizzically then decided to stop using them, which she did without a word of complaint. In fact, I cannot recall her even talking about them though she must have had severe withdrawal symptoms. I was in my mid-teens and knew about these things by this time.

After having expanded my teenage mind to encompass the entire universe, it was about time I contracted it. To let a drug such as LSD allow insights into metaphysics or to experience hallucinations so mind-bending as to alter one's perception of reality entirely is getting it to do work that the person's brain should be doing for themselves, perhaps through spiritual practices. It is not a recreational drug, especially when one's brain is not yet fully formed. And that is the same for any drug, whatever its effects. Acid gives random, sometimes terrifying realisations. To a self-obsessed burgeoning alcoholic drug addict like myself those insights drove me to become more introverted and self-centred. The only way, to my mind, out of this fearful discomfort was to take drugs that wiped out all unpleasant thoughts about me. That is where my love affair with the class of drug known as barbiturates began.

I have always had a healthy appetite, so, when someone gave me a sample of the potent sleeping capsules Seconal Sodium, bright scarlet tubes of potential unconsciousness, I took more than a healthy appetite can take. My consumption rapidly became unhealthy.

I can't recall the first time I took these potent chemicals, but I do remember that they gave me a better quality of oblivion than booze alone, which is why I took them for many years. When I awoke, whatever time that maybe, I would ingest two or three Seconal, preferably with an alcoholic drink of some kind – any kind – as alcohol potentiates barbiturates; they act on the body synergistically to produce a devastating, deadly drunkenness. The user does not know what is going on, stumbling, slurring, dribbling, eventually slipping into complete unconscious inertia. Good morning, day and everyone!

The trouble is, when I passed out, there was no guarantee I would come back to life. Barbiturates are dangerous; combined with alcohol doubly dangerous. The risk of overdose is constant; such an easy thing to achieve without even trying. The drug-induced deaths of many superstars are testimony to this.

These drugs were popular in the early 70s in my hometown and people were dying from ODs every week. Yet these 'little helpers' were easily obtainable through legitimate means. We are not talking illegal street drugs here; the most convenient way to get hold of them was by going to the doctor for a prescription. Some doctors would prescribe more readily than others and, of course, that information was freely available on the youth grapevine to which I listened.

A Scottish doctor who practised in an upmarket part of town was easy to get barbs from and would prescribe them easier if you took in a half bottle of whisky for him. If it was a female patient, he would, allegedly, feel her breasts, or whatever, which would be enough for him to hand out a prescription. His surgery was well attended for a few years until he stopped working. He was old and I guess retired. So we addicts had to find a new supplier.

A surgery close to, but on the wrong side of town, was our next destination. I recall visiting one morning finding the waiting room crammed with people I knew. It was like a reunion of the friends I hadn't seen for a while, almost like bumping into people at your friendly neighbourhood local pub, the difference being that not many of them are still alive as they were all there for the same reason as me: barbiturates. These killed a lot of those people.

My favourite was the Seconal as it got me where I wanted to be without too much heaviness. There were stronger, longer-lasting downers such as amytal, which smashed one up terrifically but caused more trouble. The mouth got too loose, too quick. Seconal seemed more manageable, so that is what I asked my doctor to prescribe for me. He was a friendly Indian chap, always eager to please, and he always pleased me because he always prescribed exactly what I asked for, no questions. He was so friendly that I once saw him driving down the main street in his golden-brown Mercedes Sport, stuck my hand out, and he stopped as a taxi would. We had a quick consultation right there at the side of the road and he handed me a private prescription for which I paid £5.

We treated the whole drug-taking thing as a joke. I boasted to my friends of this episode with the mobile doctor of death. But he was an extreme example of those days of freewheeling prescribing. Then people started dying at the rate of one or two a week.

One very popular drug had the name 'Mandrax', an extremely powerful hypnotic/sedative. In the USA one of its names had the meaning 'quiet interlude' which, for me, had a certain irony. When I took Mandies quiet moments came after I passed out. Before that point of blessed oblivion restful interludes were off the menu. I combined the tablets with alcohol, a deadly combination. Many people died from Mandrax intoxication. Those people got their supplies from doctors or from others who got them from doctors. They were prescribed in copious amounts. At one point, probably in the early seventies, they were one of the most popular drugs on the street and plentiful. I recall I had between 60 and 90 of them in my pocket when the drug squad walked through the door of the pub at which we druggies gathered. I boldly asked 'Bazil', a detective, if he would frisk me. He didn't, probably figuring that I was messing him about. I loved bluffing him; he wasn't that bright.

But I was bluffing myself. Using powerful chemicals as though they were sweeties, cramming them into my system with the insane idea that they'd make me feel better when they were actually providing a dangerous oblivion, a 'little death' every day, was a deadly pretence, a game of brinksmanship with my very life that I couldn't stop playing. I was addicted to booze and barbs. They were a way of life; at the same time, they were killing me.

As time went on the pubs we frequented got intolerant of our kind of clientele, so other establishments were found in less salubrious parts of town. I found myself one winter evening in a bar, a tiny establishment on the corner of one of many terraced streets in an area of two-up, two-down houses, when the man sitting on the bench seat next to me died. That kind of thing had become a regular occurrence and happened in the world in which I lived quite often, though not quite so personally. I can't recall if I knew the man, but, when his head flopped onto my shoulder and I, in my own chemical haze, turned to look at him, I realised that he'd left his body: there was no longer anyone at home.

Having witnessed death from overdoses before (and being hopelessly stoned myself) I took it in my stride, though the landlord of the pub was a little more worried. He, and a barfly we shall call Stan, lifted the lifeless man between them and, either side, dragged him out of the building. If there were any witnesses on the snow-covered street on this freezing night to these three they would automatically think that the one in the middle was drunk and that his friends were taking him home. Though perhaps they would find him ending up on the back of a flatbed lorry a bit harder to take. For that is where he was left, two streets away from the bar.

The coroner could not decide whether the poor fellow had died from hypothermia or from an overdose of barbiturates. But we regulars at the bar knew; yet another casualty of Seconal, Tuinal, Nembutal, or any combination thereof.

I regularly overdosed, not intentionally, but because I treated these things I got from the doctor like food. And I was an overeater. If I felt a little too conscious I took another two or three on top of the cider and earlier doses already imbibed. Unable now to remember how or in what circumstances, I often ended up in hospital having a stomach pump. A reputable doctor once showed me how many times the process had been carried out on me: 21! He then explained that having one's guts evacuated mechanically is itself a dangerous practice. But without it I could have died.

The most amazing thing about those emergency hospital visits is that I can't remember any of the stomach pumps except one, which, as I recall (unreliably perhaps), had me on all fours, being held in that position by a sort of table, bum in the air, with a tube up it, another tube down my throat expelling the contents of my belly with great force, while wearing one of those gowns that open at the back: undignified, deeply unpleasant, but life-saving.

And still, after all that, I relied on prescriptions and alcohol to help me through life. You'd think I'd learn from such extreme experiences, but I didn't know what else to do. Alcohol, illegal and prescription drugs were how I coped. The only holiday from drinking and using I got was when I went to prison, which was often.

It was during what turned out to be my final prison term that I decided to stop drinking and taking drugs. Having made this firm decision, I was released from the jail in Devon and found myself going to see Pete, a friend, who I knew would have drugs. He did, and sold some Mogadon to me, a weak prescription sleeper, but enough, along with copious amounts of cider, to give me relief from the tension and anxiety that were my constant companions. When I came round a week later, having no recollection of those seven days, I had a moment of clarity. I understood, in my heart, my powerlessness over mood-altering chemicals. This was a devastating realisation that subsequently turned out to be lifesaving.

I gave up all drugs, including alcohol, twenty-seven years ago, the day I entered a 12-Step rehab. After this I went to Alcoholics Anonymous, who saved and continue to save my life. Through their programme, I have been shown a way to live that moved me away from the person who could not stop using drugs and consuming alcohol to a life of freedom today.

What surprises me now my mind is clear, is that of the drugs I took that could have killed me, the majority were prescribed by doctors who are there to save life, not destroy it. Nevertheless, I was still able to get such deadly drugs on prescription for many years, even though it was known that I had overdosed on numerous occasions.

I thank God every day that I am a member of AA and One Day at A Time (ODAAT) follow its programme of recovery.

Chapter 20

Sarah's Story – Perfectly Broken

My name is Sarah, and I am a recovering alcoholic. My sobriety date is 11th March 2007, when I found the rooms of Alcoholics Anonymous. By then I had reached a point in my life when everything I did or ingested to relieve the way I felt had stopped working. But it had taken me a long time to realise that the mess that I was in was because I am an alcoholic and all of it was of my own making. I thought it was everyone else's fault and problem; I was just a poor persecuted soul who God and everyone else on the planet had it in for.

I was born in Alton, Hampshire to an unmarried Irish nurse and Irish doctor and was adopted three weeks later into a middle-class British family who, I have since discovered while being sober, loved me and did the best they could for me. My mother was a doctor and my father an architect; my older brother had been adopted two years previously and they gave us a loving home and as much attention as they were able in equal measure. I mention the fact that my parents loved us in equal measure because I spent my childhood with a very distorted version of this truth and spent the majority of my life, and other people's, convinced that they did not.

I had an inkling that I was somehow different from the start, but for years felt that it was because I was adopted. I have since discovered that I did not need to be adopted to feel that way at all. I remember very little of my early years, which does not make me a lot different from everyone else, but memories of family holidays are always of me standing on the sidelines afraid to join in and of being locked in the car while the rest of the family went for walks as I would refuse to go. I wanted to be as far away from other people as I could get and dreaded going on sleepovers to friends' houses, I would become so overwhelmed that I was being abandoned and get myself into such a state that my mother would have to come out in the middle of the night to collect me; life and people terrified me, and I had no idea why.

My first addiction was to books. I loved disappearing into fantasy worlds and would dream of being rescued by I don't know who or what; all I knew was that I would feel better once they did and it took a further twenty-seven years for that to happen.

I had a ferocious appetite, and my parents were always astounded at the amount I managed to consume, seeing that I was so slim. I now realise that I was burning up energy with worry and was well on the road to quite literally stuffing down any feelings I had. Running part of the school tuck shop was a perfect way to indulge my craving for sugar and I would consume four or five bars in the space of fifteen minutes on a daily basis. I had not found alcohol at this point, so food was the perfect antidote as no one seemed to think that my intake or behaviour around it was odd.

Life seemed very unfair; I did not have what other people had and certainly was not getting what I wanted. There I was, living in a beautiful five-bedroom house on the top of Richmond Hill, going on two to three holidays a year, with a pony on loan and freedom to roam; yet everything seemed against me.

I always had a feeling that life owed me, so I started thieving at an early age. It started with penny sweets from the local sweet shop, things from my brother's room or my friends' possessions. Getting away with it was fairly easy. I would just deny all knowledge if caught and the more I got a buzz out of getting away with it, the more I wanted to do it. My mother's new clothes would disappear back to the shop for a refund, and when she got wise to that and started hiding the receipts, I would still take them back and then sell the vouchers I got instead to whomever would buy them. When she stopped buying new things I moved on to her and my father's bank account, which I stole from regularly. I had complete disregard for the misery and torment I put them through. My mother only threatened me with the police once and I cannot remember why she did not follow through. I may have made one of my countless pleas and statements of remorse, which, of course, I had no intention of keeping.

At the back of my mind there was always this idea that there was something wrong with me, but I couldn't for the life of me have told you what it was, just that it was there. It was like being followed around by something that you only managed to catch a glimpse of out of the corner of your eye. My mother thought that I had a personality disorder and so sent me to a psychiatrist when I was about fourteen years old. All I remember him asking me was why I hated my family so much and me sitting in silence; that lasted three visits. I read books by Sartre and Freud thinking I would find some kind of indication to my thinking, but they just baffled me, and I remained in that state of mind for many years not knowing where or how to look for help.

I cannot remember how old I was exactly when I took my first drink, but I remember the first time it really worked for me. I was at a disco aged about fourteen and I remember feeling warm and fuzzy inside, about ten feet tall, prettier than any of the other girls in the place and capable of anything. I decided there and then that was how it should stay for the rest of my life; unfortunately it didn't. I had the classic imbalance of an ego up in the clouds and a self-worth beneath the floorboards; the only thing I found that would take this away and make me feel better was alcohol.

I had no ambition. I spent little time at school, and would persuade one of my friends to bunk off and we'd buy the cheapest, largest bottle of wine we could, of which I would drink the majority, then we'd make general nuisances of ourselves for the stallholders in Kensington Market. I thought school was for suckers and why on earth would you waste time and energy being told what to do when you could be roaming around London? Needless to say, I left with few qualifications and no intentions of getting a job. Spending time with the 'Monday Club' in my local pub was far more interesting.

From having been active growing up and able to eat what I liked with little consequence, I hadn't realised that if you stop exercising, drink alcohol regularly and eat large quantities late at night, it has a detrimental effect on your waistline. I had kind of noticed it, then not; it was the usual of something creeping up on you and before you know it, it has taken hold. My mother was quick to point it out, which I think she thought was helpful, and suggested I train to be a riding instructor, as I had always had a love of horses.

I spent six months getting up in the early hours six days a week until that became too much, and I began what became my usual walking out of work routine. I had taken slimming tablets previously, but discovered that the slimming clinic I got them from was no longer in business so I thought the best way to move the remaining excess weight I had gained in a quick and efficient manner was not to eat less and exercise more, but to take laxatives. So I duly began a regime of twenty tablets before every meal, hiding them from everybody and praying profusely that I'd make it to the toilet when the need arose, which it did, a lot!

My parents, exasperated with my lack of work ethic, kicked me out, so I moved in with my then boyfriend and soon discovered I was pregnant. I thought that if I ignored it, it would somehow go away and disappear. My partner didn't want to have a child, and not wanting to put on any more weight, or be saddled with a child on my own, I had an abortion, buried my feelings and emotions around it, split up with the guy, broke his heart, and moved back home with my tail between my legs.

I started working at a music publisher's and the scope to stay out late, drink and do as I like escalated. I loved going to awards ceremonies as they would close the whole office and I knew I didn't have to go back until the following week as they generally fell on a Friday, perfect for someone like me who would never had made it back to the office if it had been on any other day of the week. But once I was promoted, it felt like all my Christmases had come at once. I was out seeing bands, talent scouting, mixing with some not so famous musicians, staying up until all hours, which didn't feel like work at all.

My mother, who had been in and out of remission with breast cancer, was by this stage, very ill. It had spread to other areas of her body and I hated the feeling of uselessness and helplessness I had when I was with her. She spent a lot of time in hospital and I would go and sit with her during my lunch hour, wishing I had behaved better growing up and feeling as though I was the cause of her being ill. I had no idea that I wasn't an inherently bad person as my head had suggested for the past twenty-something years, nor that I was powerful enough to be the cause of someone else's illness. The only way to control these unbearable feelings and sadness was not only through alcohol, but also through food. I went on lockdown, allowing myself to eat only a small bowl of soup a day with some bread and telling my father I'd had a big lunch. As soon as I got in, I changed and headed to the pub, never once stopping to think how he may have been feeling about his wife being ill or if he would have liked some company.

My behaviour became erratic, which had nasty consequences, rows with pub drinkers resulting in the police turning up on my father's doorstep, fights with friends, mixing with unsavoury people, etc.

One evening a guy, Joe, I had seen in the pub occasionally came in. He was the cousin of a girl I went to school with and had a reputation of being a loose cannon. So much the better, I thought! There was a party that night and we ended up back at my parents' house, I had to sneak him in so that added to the excitement and risk. He told me he could kill me if he wanted to, to which I replied 'whatever'; at that point I didn't care what happened to me, so his words fell on deaf ears. However, someone I had been seeing heard I was getting involved with Joe and told me he may be HIV+.

Now most normal folk would run a mile or at least consider what they were doing for a nanosecond, but it didn't cross my mind that it was not a good idea to pursue this one. That night Joe, after a few drinks, told me his 'story', which had a tendency to frequently change, making me want him even more and sure it was my ex's way to get me back. Joe was my soulmate, and it was my fate to die the same way as him. With hindsight, I was clearly going nuts.

My mother had by this time come home and was confined to her room as the cancer had spread to her bones and skin. I, as usual, disappeared to the pub or anywhere I could go and get my hands on anything that would remove my guilt. That lovely warm feeling I had experienced in my teens and had wanted to remain with me for eternity was gone and all I wanted to do now was to numb out everything and anything. A week after my 23rd birthday my mother died. We had sat down as a family the night before with a take-away and I remember looking at her eyes and thinking that she would be dead the next day. I don't how I knew but I could just feel it. Needless to say, I behaved as I had always behaved, ran off to the pub as soon as the meal was over to the new man in my life, who clearly needed me so much more than my family, and spent the night at his. He woke me up the next morning to say there was a phone call for me. It was my brother who told me that my mother had died about an hour earlier. She had been asking for me and he had been phoning everyone he could think of to find out where I was.

The next few hours are a bit of a blur. I remember phoning friends and telling them, wanting to be anywhere else but where I was. My grandmother was in shock, as I expect you would be when you lose your only child, as were my father and brother, but again all I could think of was myself and so ran to the pub to be with those who I wanted to be with rather than with those I ought to have been.

My eating by that point had become even more erratic and I pretty much stopped altogether. Most of my sustenance, if you can call it that, came from booze. I weighed around 90 lbs and was very anaemic, I would have bouts when my blood sugar level would plummet, and I'd simply collapse in the street.

Yet I still thought I was doing OK! I thought I looked amazing; I could still attract men, even though I was with someone. I cheated with his friends, which was their problem, not mine. I had no concept of integrity, fidelity or boundaries and deluded myself into thinking that I at least had the decency to let you know that I was living with someone and if I didn't know you, well then I told you that I was with someone who was HIV+ and if you wanted to take that risk then that was your prerogative. My conscience was clear on that front. I was as honest as the day was long, or so I thought. What I didn't tell them was that during the eight years I was with Joe we used protection on just two occasions; it is only by the grace of God I didn't contract it and pass it on.

There was a nagging feeling in the back of my head that kept telling me that I would die if I stayed in London, so I decided to get out. I latched on to an Australian girl who worked at the pub and was about to go travelling. Dad was there to fund it, well, why wouldn't he be? He wanted me to sort myself out, didn't he? I had lost my job at the music publishers by this time. 'Not turning up and treating it like a holiday camp' was how they put it in my dismissal letter. Didn't they understand my mother had recently died? What was the matter with these people?! My father bought me my ticket, probably more to get rid of me for a while than anything else, and said he would transfer some money to my account. Finally, I felt some hope that life was going to get better.

The money my father was meant to transfer didn't come through and I went and wailed to a family friend, who lent me some to start me off until it did. I gave no thought to working and saving for this trip. That hadn't even crossed my mind once.

So off we went to Turkey and things quietened down. I felt better, the bad consequences stopped happening, and I was enjoying the sunshine and meeting new people and seeing new sights. Next stop was Israel. We planned to work on a kibbutz for a couple of months and then move on to Egypt. It was pretty basic; the work was monotonous and with the same people day in, day out. The consequences which had disappeared at the beginning crept back in and now there was nowhere to hide. It got to the point when I made everyone angry having broken into a bar and allowed the blame to fall on others.

I headed to Eilat, broke and unable to get to Cairo for my flight. My father had long since washed his hands of me and his parting words during our last conversation were, "Why don't you get yourself a job?" The old resolve of 'I'll show you' returned and I found work on a day boat. There I met an American woman who asked if I knew anyone who was looking for work on a dive boat, I jumped at the chance. I lasted six weeks, spending the majority of the time drunk or smoking opium with other deckhands. My enthusiasm for the job waned and I decided it was time to head home.

Travelling back, I resolved that everything was going to be different. I wasn't going to get involved with anyone. Joe had been sectioned while I was away, so I certainly didn't want to see him, and looking for work was going to be my focus as well as rebuilding my relationship with my father. How wrong could I be? Where had been my high resolve?

When I got home, I couldn't get in and headed straight for the pub. There I bumped into one of Joe's friends, who promptly passed on to him that I was back. I then went home to fill my father in on my trip, but within two hours I was back in the pub with Joe and right back where I left off. The consequences got worse again, and my father threw me out. I moved around friends' places, then persuaded Joe to let me move in.

Six years of chaos followed, including stays in police cells, infidelity and violence. I fell in and out of jobs, drank alcoholically, and took illegal drugs every day, and my eating went off the wall again. Joe was prescribed sleeping tablets which I would take as soon as I woke up in order to knock me out again. My father disowned me and crossed the road if he saw me coming.

I then had what is called a moment of desperation and asked for help. I had just come out of blackout and found myself standing in front of a desk sergeant being charged with assault with a knife. I was asked if I wanted to make a phone call and I said I wanted to call my partner. The police officer informed me that that wasn't possible as he was the victim. I remembered my brother's telephone number and he collected me from court the next morning and took me to his house. I had managed to hide a lot of what I was getting up to from him and my father, but they decided that enough was enough and moved me into my brother's. A year previously, my grandmother had died and left us all some money. I managed to keep hold of all of mine, mainly because I wasn't going to let Joe get his hands on it, my attitude having been what was his was mine and what was mine was mine too.

We all pooled our money and bought a flat in which I was to live. I was very unhappy and extremely ungrateful as, a) it was nowhere near my usual haunts, even though I was banned from most of them, and b) was too close to my family's prying eyes. Despite my protestations, I moved in, got a job and a new circle of friends.

I started going to the gym six or seven times a week, sometimes twice a day, and my food was back on lockdown. I wouldn't eat after a certain hour or mix certain food; it all had to be weighed and definitely nothing sweet! I was constantly on high alert and my behaviour around men got out of control as I put myself in more stupid situations. I managed to live like that for a few more years. It's extraordinary how I convinced myself that if the outside looks OK, then everything else must be too. But that wasn't the truth; I was completely numb inside, had no empathy with or for others and had totally shut down.

When I was 35, I went to Ireland to stay with my dad and stepmother. My father didn't know what to do with me as my mood swings were even more erratic. I finally broke down and told my stepmother that I was pregnant.

I thought long and hard about keeping it, but the thought of having to bring up a child on my own horrified me. There was no way I was going to be a single mother. I was swayed between feelings of utter sadness and love for what was growing inside of me and of complete selfishness of how this would affect me, my body, and more importantly, when would I drink, even though I hadn't stopped drinking. So, another trip to the abortion clinic, but then it dawned on me that whilst I wasn't getting pregnant all the time, I was ending up with inappropriate men and a pattern was emerging that I got into trouble when I drank. I hung on to the hope that things would change while doing nothing to implement that for a further year and then something shifted.

I went to see my GP and for the first time was honest about the amount I was drinking, although I still distorted the truth. He prescribed anti-depressants and told me not to drink on them. I lasted three months and started to feel better physically, thinking I'd cracked it. I decided my life was missing that all-important ingredient of a relationship, so I manipulated an ex's number from my brother and met up with him.

Unsurprisingly, we went to a pub. I told him I wasn't drinking and sat in the most excruciating paranoia and discomfort, thinking everyone was talking about me. A thought flew into my mind. It was as though I went into automatic pilot. 'I'll just have one, that will take the edge off.' So, I had one, followed by a few more, and was quickly back where I started.

A Jungian therapist I had begun to see had been drip-feeding me about my drinking and also about AA, but I hadn't heard any of it. It was Christmas 2006 and I had gone to a friend's birthday party, armed with the knowledge that I had a drink problem. This caused a depression, and I spent the evening feeling sorry for myself, telling my woes to anyone who would listen and drinking copious amounts of coffee. I now understand that just because you know something, it doesn't change anything unless you follow it with action, which, of course, I did not do. So, it didn't take me long to pick up alcohol again.

One of my therapist's patients, who was in AA, agreed to meet me. She gave me a list of local meetings, but I was always far too busy doing nothing to go. It got to the stage when it was more my mental state that was driving me nuts rather than having to lose everything. I finally found the courage to pick up the phone and the identification was instantaneous. I had suspicions my therapist passed on information about me to this woman, but now I know how AA works I know she had not; one sober alcoholic passes on to a newcomer their experiences. She asked me if I wanted to go to a meeting and I umed and ahed. She said she went regularly and if I wanted to come we could also go for coffee afterwards. I put it off for a while longer and then woke up one morning and realised that 'this' was the day and there was no turning back.

Walking to that meeting and allowing myself to ask for help were two of the hardest things I have ever done. I now know they were two of the bravest and the best. I have since been given a life I never knew existed. While certain areas of my external life have changed less, the inward part of me has been transformed. I live the majority of the time in a state of relative peace and calmness I had never experienced before, and the amazing thing is that by just showing up for life, thanks to the AA programme it gets better and better. It's not without its challenges, sadness and tears, but it is real, and I get to experience all of the good stuff alongside the bad and stay sober, just by following a few simple suggestions and trying the best I can to help others. Sobriety has also become a great healer, not just for me but for my relationships with others. My father and I have a very strong bond these days and I am blessed and grateful that he is in my life,

I would not change where I have been and certainly not where I am now for anything as I truly believe that I have finally moved myself out of the way to allow God's grace to enter and touch my soul.

Chapter 21

To be gay or not to be gay.

Being an addict is the one fact above all others that has defined my life. Never being comfortable in my own skin, always wanting more, never feeling that I am enough.

Was I born an addict, or did I become an addict at some indiscernible point during my life? The answer to that question is of course immaterial, what is important is that once an addict always an addict. Acceptance, if only of that fact, can provide the key to freedom and a passport to a better life.

I am now 60 years old and have been clean and sober since I was 29. In that time, one day at a time, through an ongoing application of the Steps ('How It Works'), primarily through going to meetings, having a sponsor and occasionally thinking of someone other than myself, my inner world has continued to evolve and change – sometimes I can look at the outside world and find it and me deeply unsatisfactory.

It is when I look within with the help of the 12 Steps that I have been able to make some sense of my life, find a connection to a higher power, some meaning and crucially a primary purpose – this precious thing called life that I played Russian roulette wheel and that by the age of 29 had become such a burden that I could not handle it without ingesting increasingly large amounts of life-threatening substances.

I AM AN ADDICT!

One of the other great and seminal discoveries I made when I got clean and eventually started to awaken from my life fuelled by drugs and alcohol was that I was Gay!

Was I born that way? Again it matters not. What does matter is I stayed clean and had an awakening!

When I was just eight I was sent to an all-boys boarding school. Part of me loved it and part of me hated it, but from the youngest age I can remember being sexually attracted to other boys.

I started smoking at a very young age and was generally very naughty and also had a fixation for alcohol. Certainly from the age of 10 I was sexually obsessed. I masturbated the whole time and had crushes on other boys. One boy, let's call him Bill, I fell in love with - I didn't know it at the time but when I left that school aged 12 I remember pining for him and wishing that I could to spend the whole of my life with him.

There was through all this though a real innocence – I carried no shame about anything as far as I can recall. From the age of 10 I smoked my mother's cigarettes at home and left then in an ashtray by my bed. It never occurred to me to hide them, although of course I got into trouble. My older brother who was then 17 smoked so why shouldn't I?

Bill and I were both good at sport and we were singled out by the master who took the First XI football team for special attention. He was kind and funny and gave us and other boys sweets and to some beer. One day he asked me if Bill and I would like to come to his room where he lived within the school grounds. Bizarrely even then if I could have a beer then I would do anything.

Bill and I would have sex with each other whilst he watched. I adored Bill and I liked beer, so it seemed like a good arrangement. We were 11/12 years old, just naughty boys unencumbered by guilt or shame.

However dark clouds started to descend. The master warned us that if anyone found out about what we had been doing, our parents would inevitably find out and we would probably go to prison. Prison, that was scary and of course we had no way of knowing the truth. So fear, guilt and shame took a front seat in my life. I learnt to lie to myself and others.

The feelings I had for Bill were obviously wrong and more than that could land me in jail, and for an addict like me they became inadvertently the spark that led to 17 years of being 'straight'. Until I got clean I never again had any sexual contact with another boy.

Aged 13 I left that school and went to my big school, I loved it. I was popular, I good at sport, bone idle academically but was always up for fun and fun always involved smoking and drinking and eventually drugs.

My life at that school until I got clean aged 29 was that of a heterosexual man. Of course I sometimes found other boys attractive, but I put that down to being the fault of the master who had abused me. He'd queered me up! Perfect rationalisation.

Never once can I remember ever thinking I am gay or indeed different from any of my peers. Now I may not be the brightest person in the world, but the power of denial aided and abetted by alcohol and drugs enabled me to believe with all my heart that I was straight.

I had many girlfriends; sex was good but never great and always fuelled by copious amounts of drugs and alcohol – is it any wonder none of the relationships lasted? I was bewildered by life; I was looking back terrified of girls and terrified of the idea of having a wife and children. But the desire to fit in and be like everybody else was everything.

My last girlfriend who I was with for several years, not without various separations eventually left me for good. She could not cope with my drinking and drug use. She thought I might get my shit together if we got married. We had discussed it but I just knew that I was so messed up that I could not look after myself let alone anyone else, so I said no and she left.

Her parting shot to me was 'What the hell is the matter with you, are you gay?' I was 28 and hadn't had any sexual contact with a boy since I was 13, what on earth can she mean?

The last year of my using was the worst because I knew that I was killing myself and a part of me wanted to stop. I was not an addict though not that I knew anything about addiction, and I knew absolutely nothing about recovery.

So by mid October 1989 my girlfriend had left, I had destroyed my business, my money was running out and my father in particular was totally distraught by so much of my reckless behaviour. Whilst my parents knew I drank a lot they knew nothing of the various drug habits that were destroying my life and on which I spent everything I had.

I then made a Faustian pact with drugs and alcohol. If I was still alive on January 1st, 1990, I would stop taking drugs and drinking. I did not do that because I thought I was an alcoholic or an addict or that I needed to join NA/AA, which I was not even aware existed, I did it because I hated myself and was losing the will to live.

To cut a long story short from October 1989 to January 1st, 1990, I used and drank everything I could - the brakes were off – I was determined to give drugs and alcohol every last chance to work. So when I woke up or more accurately regained consciousness on January 1st feeling like shit that was it. Amazingly I have not used a drug or drunk alcohol since that day. So began my journey into what I came to know as 'Recovery'.

It was not of course all plain sailing. After two months of being clean and sober during which time I was introduced to NA/AA meetings I decided that although I probably was an addict and an alcoholic and I did want to stay clean, my real problem was that I was insane. I was also still thinking that a lot of money and a girlfriend was what I really needed; just getting clean and sober had not made me honest even about something as seminal as my sexuality.

After two months my life without drugs and without any programme left me feeling suicidal, totally paralysed with fear, so I checked myself into a psychiatric hospital, which also had an addiction unit.

I was there for three months, and I came out fully convinced of two really important things, first that I really really am an addict and secondly in order to stay clean and get well I needed to go to meetings. I was still in total denial about my sexuality although I had begun to talk about my confusion around it, which in itself was a breakthrough.

After nearly a year of being in recovery I found myself in Paris with a gay friend in recovery, who was working there for a couple of days. He thought I was straight. Whilst he worked in the evening I went to an AA meeting where I met an American guy. We went out to dinner after the meeting. He came back with me to my hotel. He was gay and asked me if I was gay. I said that I didn't know!

He stayed the night with me. I woke up the next morning in bed with him and felt a peace that I had never felt before, being there with him felt like the most natural thing in the world. Oh my God I am gay!

I told my friend what had happened, and I was then able to tell my family that I was gay; I knew that if I didn't get honest my chances of staying clean and certainly being happy would be slim to none. The sad thing was even though I was able to tell people there was still a big part of me that didn't want to be gay. The pride had to go, or I would never be able to find the peace of mind and serenity that people talked of and that seemed like distant foreign lands.

Being an addict and being gay for me are the same - I either am or I am not as I was told it is better to be in recovery pretending that I am addict than not in recovery pretending that I am not and so it was and is with being gay.

When I told my sister that I was gay she didn't care at all, but I still said to her that I wished that I wasn't. It took me to work the steps with my sponsor to really begin to feel comfortable about who I was. Self-acceptance is the key, and that is what I found and continue to find in meetings, with my friends in recovery in particular who understand the insanely savage depths of self-hatred that can always drive my thinking if left untreated for any length of time.

The fact that I didn't die before I found my real self in recovery is proof to me that I have a higher power. Recovery found me, everything I have has been achieved by me getting my out of the way. Drugs enabled me to pretend to be who I wanted to be, but never who I actually was.

Reality can be a very rude awakening but it's a lot less bumpy in the long run. Better to be awake for one's life than merely a semi-conscious passenger. So the job is to awaken and then stay awake! God knows I don't need to drink or take drugs to be delusional!

God bless recovery, God bless the fellowships and God bless all my fellow travellers.

Chapter 22

Stephen's Story

I was born in north London, the last of five brothers and two younger sisters. My parents were from the Caribbean and I grew up in a mixed community. For the first ten years of my life my father worked away as an engineer and came home at weekends, so my mother looked after the children. Because there were seven of us, she could not cope. My brothers were up to all sorts of criminal activities, getting arrested by the police a lot of the time. Having to go to police stations and courts with my brothers wore my mother and father down, and in the end my four brothers were taken into care. So I was brought up in chaos and had a chaotic family life.

I found it exciting when my brothers were home and they talked about getting up to no good. I was much more interested in that than being at school with my peers, so that was the route I chose to pursue.

I do remember being quite fearful as a young boy; in particular I was afraid of the dark, authority and my father – who I had seen punish my brothers physically since I was two.

It was not long before I began stealing and committing petty crimes. I started to receive punishments from the police, my father and authority, but I thought that was all cool because my brothers were doing it. I didn't realise until later that I was doing this to get the respect of my brothers – this is called 'people pleasing' – and it was the reason I did most things at the time. All in all, I now see I was leading a thoroughly dishonest life.

There were no signs of alcoholism or drug addiction in my family at this time, but I was about to change all that, as was my father.

One summer, when I was about twelve, I went to the carnival in Notting Hill and met up with some of my brothers' friends. They took me around with them all day, stealing, and at the end we went to a night club – it was a café, really, a notorious meeting place in Harlesden High Street for local villains on Saturday evenings, and only one hundred yards from the police station. So they got to know me, and I got to know them quite well. Someone gave me a joint for the first time and I remember the feeling it gave me; it was wonderful, the equivalent to having my first drink.

When I was younger my father gave me Babycham, which made me feel high. I didn't know it was alcohol, but I would always feel relaxed when I drank it and the few drags on the joint made me feel the same: elated and confident. I could even talk to girls as I was normally a very shy kid.

By the age of thirteen I was addicted to pot and smoked it every day without fear. I would go to bed late, wake up late and not go to school. I would go stealing so I could buy cannabis. This way of life took me to a young offenders' institute when I was fourteen. I carried on like this until I was sixteen, when I started having panic attacks every time I smoked, so I decided to stop. I then had mental withdrawals on and off for a couple of years, which I did not know were caused by my giving up weed. I simply thought I was going crazy. Then I found alcohol could replace this and I felt fine again.

I was very much a binge drinker and would go for days, even weeks, without alcohol, but when I did drink I always got drunk. By this time, my father was also binge drinking, which made my drinking seem acceptable.

In my mid-teens I became a high standard junior athlete playing tennis for my county and representing England in International Federation junior tournaments. Also, I came out of drama school with a First Class degree at twenty- four, so there were times I felt pretty good about myself. As I look back I remember that when I had been at drama school, most of the three years I was there I did not drink.

I then went into the acting profession and, because I was considered to have a lot of potential, I was able to get a top agent. Almost immediately I got a lot of work and made good money. I had a flat near St James's Park, not far from Buckingham Palace, which gave me easy access to London's West End and its theatres.

Everything was fine for the first year I was there, until one day after work in a nightclub one of my friends gave me a line of cocaine and from that moment on I was caught up in a new addiction and the chaos this causes. As this crept up on me it was hardly noticeable, but as the overall experience took over my life the outcome was inevitable. It was probably unnoticeable, though, because I was becoming more and more successful in the theatre, films and TV.

By now, every time I had alcohol I would want more and that would lead me to cocaine and, very occasionally, ecstasy, which I was always able to get through contacts. And the nature of these drugs enabled me to drink three times as much as I could normally drink. It had not disrupted my work yet, but it was messing with my relationships with girlfriends. I always wanted to be out drinking and doing drugs, fooling around with other women, and then the next day I would feel guilty and hungover and want to kill myself.

I decided – or I should say my partner decided – it would be best if I moved from the flat near St James's Park, so I bought a flat as far from Central London as seemed sensible; but other than the geography, not much changed. I carried on the same behaviour as before. Then we had a baby daughter and I thought the best thing would be for me to move out of London altogether. My thinking was that this would focus me on being a good father and partner. So we moved to a leafy part of the Midlands in Warwickshire.

Things were fine for a while until I started to drink again. Before I knew it I had found a drug dealer and was doing exactly the same things I had been doing in London. I then started to want to be in London when I was in our new home, and in Warwickshire when I was in London, so I would drive down to London after a drug-fuelled argument with my partner, check into a hotel and drink and do drugs for three or four days, then go home in a terrible state.

By now I was barred from most of my favourite bars and clubs because I was aggressive when under the influence. Also, all this driving to and fro when I was drunk and high meant I knew I was living dangerously. So, one day, after a binge weekend, I went to see my doctor and he told me to go to Alcoholics Anonymous, at which I turned my nose up. Then he referred me to the Alcoholics Advisory Service, where I saw a counsellor in alcoholism and heavy drinking. I was told straight away I was not an alcoholic and that my career was the problem due to the hours I worked. So I carried on drinking and the outcome got worse, especially when my father died from alcoholism.

From then on things changed, and although it did not happen immediately, my father's death did speed up the process. I was still drinking and drugging, but not enjoying it at all and it was now getting noticeable at work. Also, I got arrested for being drunk and disorderly, threatening behaviour, and once for possession of drugs. Blackouts were also frequent. I told my partner that if I didn't sort myself out, I would admit myself into a treatment centre. That day did come, but when I rang the counsellor from the Alcoholics Advisory Service to arrange it, he said I wasn't bad enough. This spurred me to ring AA.

A woman answered the AA telephone helpline and I told her my story. Somehow I connected with her – she was seven years sober and told me I needed to go to an AA meeting and that she would send someone around to take me. A fellow called Bill with ten years sobriety showed up and took me to a meeting in the Midlands. I identified with almost all that was said there, particularly some stuff the main speaker shared about fear, and when people shared back on the same subject, it felt like I was in the right place. But after six months I drank again; and this time the effects and consequences were even worse.

I managed to get myself back ten months later. This time I was completely broken and willing to do what I was told. So I got a sponsor who suggested I go to 90 meetings in 90 days and work the steps. I had done none of these three things the first time I came in, so it had only been a matter of time before I got drunk again.

I have now been sober in AA for eighteen years and the results have been fantastic. I still go to several meetings a week and now have sponsees. I was told that helping others would help me, so that is what I do. I also do service at meetings and talk to my sponsor regularly, especially when I need help, which still occurs. I pray in the mornings and at night. I read the AA books *Alcoholics Anonymous* and *As Bill Sees It*. I go to Step meetings and life has become a gift instead of a chore. Other benefits are that I enjoy my work much more, I am a good father, son and brother, and my relationship with my daughter's mother is excellent. I am also a good friend, and from feedback, I am told I am a very good actor. I also have a partner whom I adore.

I can honestly say that all aspects of my life have changed for the better since my drinking, drugging days, and all this has been down to Alcoholics Anonymous. But most of all, I have peace of mind, as do my family.

Chapter 23

Holly's Story of Alcohol and Love Addiction

My dad did not really want me. He had asked my mum to wait to get pregnant until he knew if he was going on a tour of duty with the RAF. But she did not. He was posted to an island in the Indian Ocean soon after I was born. I lived a blissful early life in the loving care of my mum and grandparents. It was a caring home, free from any form of abuse. But that ended when my dad returned. After a year and a half away, I was an unwelcome obstacle sitting between him and his wife. He must have felt an outsider – here was this family unit, happy and cosy, and he felt left out. I'm told I was scared of him. Not surprising really. He worked hard to reclaim his position, telling my mum I'd been spoiled and needed disciplining. I was two years old and being slapped for my misdemeanors.

As I grew up my dad punished me for almost everything; for bad table manners, shouting, arguing, annoying him, annoying my mum. Anything. My sister came along when I was two and a half and she became the 'good girl'. I knew I was bad. I was told I was. I was told I was 'not normal' and that I was 'trying to come between my mum and dad'. I was also told I was 'evil'. My dad hit me a fair bit. And the worst part was being shut in my room – crying for my mum. But she never came. He would not let her. I grew up worried that people would never like me or love me because they would eventually see through to the 'evil' inside me. I had few friends, not wanting anyone to get close enough to know me. I feared the rejection that would inevitably come.

So I knew what my problem was. Me. I was an unlovable, abnormal, evil girl. But at five years old, I found my solution. I was given a glass of Babycham at my aunt's wedding. I was a bridesmaid and loved the attention. The alcohol made me buzz with excitement. I felt pretty, vivacious and lovable. I went round the room taking sips of everyone's drinks and lapping up the attention I was getting. 'She's so much better when she's drunk,' someone said. Yes, of course I was. The drink took me out of the self I loathed. The me that everyone hated.

I started drinking properly at 15. It made me feel 'normal', smoothed the way to go to parties, to chat to boys. And boys were what I wanted. Or a boyfriend. I wanted to be loved. I found a lovely boy and took him hostage for two years. I was a binge drinker during this time. Whenever I took a drink I could not stop. I drank to blackout. At my 16th birthday party I passed out before most of the guests arrived. My dad dragged me by the feet into the dining room and left me there for the duration of the party.

My parents drank a fair bit – home brew was all the rage. Drinking was approved of and they positively encouraged me to get drunk because they said I was much better when I'd had a drink, more 'normal'. So my teenage years were pretty drunken, and I progressed to daily drinking. I was arrested a couple of times for stealing booze and fags, but overnight stays in police cells were not enough to deter me from drinking. I moved on another boyfriend/hostage – handpicked for his drinking ability. I took drugs now and again, mainly because a line or two of cocaine or speed would enable me to drink a lot more and last a lot longer.

Despite being quite bright, I did not do well at school, so ended up at the local art college. This was a good move as drinking was tolerated. And it led to a job in one of the booziest professions out there – advertising. And so the drinking continued and escalated as I mixed with big-time London ad agency drinkers. And I became promiscuous. The boyfriend was left behind as I drank after work in pubs and bars. Sometimes I ended up in a strange flat with a strange man. On one occasion the bed was wet. I felt such shame. I was increasingly feeling suicidally ashamed. I was waking up with severe hangovers every day and dragging myself to work. I knew it had to stop. Not the drinking, of course. The men bit. I had to find a way to drink and be safe. So I took another hostage, who eventually became my husband.

I wanted to change myself, change my life and be accepted and approved of. So what would help? I know – have a baby! So I did. And then I had another. And another. And another. I had four babies in five years. Each time I thought the pregnancy and the baby would fix me and stop me drinking. But of course, they didn't. I controlled my drinking during the pregnancies but was back on it straight away afterwards.

So everything changed, but nothing changed. I knew I had a problem, but I also had other problems. And I needed drink to help me. It helped me after a stressful day at work, a hard day with the kids, a good day at work, a good time with the kids. And so it went on. For years. I regularly drove drunk with my kids and other people's kids in the car. I became fiercely ambitious for my kids, controlling every aspect of their lives. They could not just do a drama club, they had to be on the West End stage; playing sport was not enough – it had to be county or national level or I wasn't satisfied. I boasted about them constantly, using their achievements to prove my success as a mother. But all the time I wasn't a good mother.

My sons hated me drinking. One of them used to try taking the glass from my hand. I would scream and shout at him. I'd often go to bed in blackout, sometimes not remembering if I'd cooked them any dinner. My husband also drank heavily, and we would sometimes do a booze cruise to France. We'd buy so many cases of wine that when we piled them in the car there was hardly room for all the boys. We'd squash them in amongst the boxes to endure an uncomfortable journey back across the Channel.

My behaviour began to get worse. I wrecked dinner parties, barbecues and family events. I had to take a back door exit from a family wedding because I'd propositioned the priest and said all sorts of inappropriate things to people. I realised I had to find help when, after a drunken night out (where I'd ended up in a lap-dancing club and a brothel) I was in a state on the Tube and a stranger called my husband to pick me up. I couldn't even tell them where I needed to get off. My husband collected me and left me in the car on the drive all night. And then, a few weeks later, the same thing happened again. I promised my husband I would find a way to control my drinking. This is what I tried.

I asked a hypnotherapist to hypnotise me to drink only six glasses of wine. I bought only very expensive wine, tried counselling, tried not starting drinking until after 7 p.m. and then I went to see a very expensive alcohol specialist at a posh clinic. He said if I did not stop drinking like I was I would be dead in five years. But he said that if I proved I could control it I would be fine, and I wouldn't need AA.

This stark fact did not deter me; in fact, it made me cover up my drinking. I lied to the psychiatrist – and he believed me. So I carried on, but hid the amount from my family. But then came the moment I surrendered. We'd been to a neighbour's barbecue and I'd behaved badly. When I came home, my son then aged fifteen, videoed me as I came through the door. The next day I woke with a suicidal hangover and my son showed me the video. It was horrendous. My dress was ripped, and I'd lifted my skirt to flash myself to the camera. It was truly disgusting. My son pleaded with me to stop drinking. Later that day I phoned the AA helpline.

The next evening I met a woman outside a meeting. I was convinced the room would be full of losers and I would not fit in. I was pretty arrogant, telling the woman I was 'just seeing what it was like'. But the main share literally told my story. An AA cliché, I know, but I identified 100% and ended up sharing back. After the meeting, a group of women scooped me up and I have not had a drink since that day. That is eleven years ago.

I got a sponsor after a few weeks and went to 90 meetings in 90 days as suggested. While my first thought was that my life would be over when I stopped drinking, it really had only just begun. Another AA cliché is that 'putting down the drink is the easy bit' – and it is absolutely true. While it is very, very hard, it was not as difficult as dealing with the real underlying problem; myself. You see I'd thought drink had stopped being my solution and had become my problem. But it wasn't, it was still my solution. The problem was and is me.

With my sponsor I started going through the steps. But being an alcoholic, my self-will continued to cause me to pursue other ways of 'fixing myself'. I had always been a spender. Spending money made me feel powerful and the things I could buy made me feel good. I once had a swimming pool put in, even though I hate swimming. I just wanted the status of having one to sit round with a glass of wine in my hand of course. So, at the end of my first year I triumphantly picked up my 1-year medal but was a wreck inside. I had what they called an 'emotional rock bottom'. If I was going to get well, I had to get honest. I had to admit to the spending and the remortgaging. I was in a mess at work; I had lost my job. I got another one and lost that. I needed to get humble, get on my knees and work on my character defects. So I got a new sponsor and went through the steps again. I also recognised my cross-addictions and worked the programme on those too. I became willing to trust in a 'higher power'. I was not the most powerful thing in the universe. There obviously is something out there more powerful than me. Even if it is a force of nature, or humanity itself.

The AA programme has helped me understand myself and how I work. It's not psychoanalysis – it's a practical way to accept the way I am. And it gave me the tools to deal with 'life on life's terms'.

A lot has happened in the eleven years since I stopped drinking. My marriage did not survive me getting sober – I changed too much. I suffer guilt and shame over this and have to continually use the programme to help me come to terms with it. I have moved home several times, changed careers and had disastrous affairs with unsuitable men. My problems with sex and relationships became worse in sobriety. I used men to 'fix' me, and sex to give me the excitement I felt I needed. My experience in AA helped me see what was happening, but I chose to join another fellowship to help me work on these specific issues. Sex and Love Addicts Anonymous, SLAA, helped me to work the steps in a different way, addressing my addiction to sex and love rather than to alcohol.

Thanks to AA and SLAA, despite having my heart broken and my life turned upside-down several times, I did not drink. I got through the pain using my higher power, the AA and SLAA programmes, and the support of the amazing and wonderful friends I met in these two fellowships.

I now have pretty decent relationships with my four sons, one of whom is in recovery as well, but I still struggle with my parents. AA has shown me I can get through anything – and from pain comes growth. And I am growing every day.

Chapter 24

Alan an English Family man's Story

My name is Alan, and I am an alcoholic. I got sober in 1990 and have remained abstinent since. As I write my story I have over thirty years' continuous sobriety, which is the result of working the 12-step programme of Alcoholics Anonymous and the loving guidance of former alcoholics who had already followed this path.

To begin, I need to share a bit about my early family life. I am one of seven children who grew up in Colne, a small Lancashire mill town where there was a lot of poverty. I had a loving mother, but my father had a severe drink problem and wasn't employed most of the time, so in our household there wasn't much love or money.

In my early days I remember we couldn't afford school uniforms. My mother had to use tokens which you took to the Co-op to exchange for clothes, which everybody knew were government low-grade items. We also had to have free school dinners, so, from a very early age I was set apart from most of the children.

I always felt different, like I did not belong; even from my brothers and sisters I felt disconnected. I also had severe learning difficulties, and from six to eleven years old, I went to several different junior schools because of my dysfunctional behaviour in the classroom. I then went to High School and failed the 11+. Because of my reading and writing difficulties, I was put in the remedial department, which was separated from the main school. Being put in this 'special' category meant I was ridiculed, which added to the feeling that I was different and that nobody understood. So I started to become a loner aged twelve.

I was also bullied, until one day, when one of the hardest boys in the school targeted me, I went into a rage and was very violent towards him. From then on, I got respect and a reputation, as everyone knew I would react with violence if I was picked on.

I started drinking alcohol at the age of fourteen. From day one it was a problem and I had blackouts. Aged fifteen, I was asked to leave school because of my behaviour. I had no qualifications and was too young to start work, so I just stayed at home. I drank as often as possible and, as a consequence, did things that were not good. At the age of sixteen, I was offered a job in a local weaving mill as a general labourer. I began by sweeping the floor and carrying rolls of fabric. This meant I now had money to spend on alcohol.

I got arrested for the first time when I was sixteen for being drunk and disorderly at a stag party in Blackpool. I went into a blackout and woke in a police cell. I was released later that day and got a train home. On the train, I met the men who had been at the stag party. They congratulated me on being a hard man and told me they were proud of me. It left me thinking that getting drunk, into a fight and arrested was good for my reputation and people wouldn't ridicule me.

I had other drink-related run-ins with the police for criminal damage, drunk and disorderly, and serious actual bodily harm, when a landlady and landlord got injured. In that case I was lucky not to go to prison.

I met my first wife when I was sixteen. She worked in the mill where I was labouring. She was four years older than me, and when I was seventeen she became pregnant. We decided to get married and did so two days after my eighteenth birthday. Three months later our son was born. He was a beautiful baby, but by my twentieth birthday the marriage was over because I didn't know how to be a father or husband, and by then alcohol had become my main focus. Before I went to work I went to the pub, and when I finished I went to the pub. When my wife left me to live with someone else, it gave me the opportunity to drink even more and I went further downhill.

I asked my mum and dad if I could live with them, but they said there was no way I could go back there with my type of behaviour. So I stayed in the marital home, even though my wife had taken everything except a bed. All I did now was go to work and get drunk. During this time, I was violent towards one of my brothers and father, each time caused by drinking. I was always remorseful and promised never to do it again. I would try to be a loving son and brother but every time I picked up a drink, I lost control. All the time my drinking was getting worse.

Aged twenty, I met my second wife. She was four years younger than me and fell in love with me, seeing me as this tough 'Jack the Lad' character. Two years later she became pregnant, so we got married. I asked her parents, but they didn't want anything to do with me because they knew I was an alcoholic. Even my father told her it was a bad idea to marry me! Soon after our son was born my alcoholism began to affect us as a family: again, I wasn't a good father or husband. We had two more children and by the time the second was born we lived in poverty. There were many occasions when I'd come home drunk, smash furniture and blame my wife. I always blamed somebody else, but underneath I was ashamed. I frequently promised I would never do it again, but then I'd always have another drink. When I went out and started drinking, I couldn't stop. I didn't know I was an alcoholic and different from other people.

Sometimes I wouldn't go home for two or three days. I would wake up in blackout not knowing where I was, what I'd done, or how I'd got there. On one occasion I went out on a Friday night and arrived home on the Sunday in a suit two sizes too small for me. Apparently, I'd been to a wedding. Someone had lent me a suit and I'd spent the weekend in blackout. My wife and children had no idea where I was.

Somehow, I kept my job, even though many times I fell out with colleagues, and management used to just look at me in disbelief; I caused damage and wasn't a nice person. By this time my brothers and sisters and my wife's family distanced themselves from me. They even sent clothes to us because most of my money went on alcohol. I started getting violent towards my wife. On one occasion I woke up and she had a black eye. I vowed I would not do it again, but I did. By now, if I picked up a drink, I had no control over where it would lead.

I was scared if I drank, I was scared if I didn't drink. As the years went on my behaviour got worse and I knew if I didn't stop I was going to lose all my family, my children, and end up in prison, a mental institution or dead. These were the only options my thirty-one-year-old brain told me I had.

One night I went to a nightclub. On my way home I went into the mill car park where I used to work and had recently left. I knew I was beaten by alcohol and began to cry. I pleaded to whatever God there was to stop me hurting those I loved; all I wanted was to be a good father, husband, for people to respect me, and not live this awful life. I know I then went home but I can't remember what happened when I got there. I was in a blackout that went on for three days.

On the Sunday morning I woke up and saw broken furniture in the bedroom. My wife wasn't there. I was full of fear, scared of what I was going to find in the rest of the house. I heard a noise in the attic, left the bedroom, and went upstairs. There I saw my wife and three young boys sitting on the bed, huddled together scared of me, scared of their father. I saw the pain; I saw the fear and the only thing I could think to do was to go and have a drink.

I went into a few pubs and in one the landlord said, 'Alan, you don't look right.' He got a bottle of beer out of the fridge, opened it and put it on the bar. He said, 'You can have this one on me.'

I looked at it almost paralysed. After a few ashamed, terror-filled moments, I said, 'I don't want it.'

I turned around and walked out. I haven't had a drink of alcohol from that day to this.

On the 13th October 1990, after what transpired to have been an horrendous weekend for my family, I knew my drinking was over. On the Monday morning I phoned the local helpline of AA in Manchester. I soon got a call from a man named Bill. He told me he was an alcoholic and I could get help if I needed it. Three days later he met me outside my first AA meeting. I was terrified. I didn't know what to expect. I just knew I had to do something about my drinking.

There were several people sitting around a table. Someone made me a cup of tea. Another startled me when he said, 'I wondered when you'd get here, Alan.' I later found out this was because I was well-known in Colne for getting drunk. Someone else said, 'Alan, because you're a newcomer, you're the most important person here. You need never drink again if you don't want to.' Then he added that I could have a good life, which was so much what I wanted.

Before I left, I was given an AA Starter Pack. When I got home, I opened it and found several pamphlets; one of which had twenty simple questions regarding alcoholism. My answers made clear that I was an alcoholic. I said to my wife that I was going to quit drinking for good. She looked at me and said, 'Alan, I've heard that so many times.' But I knew something was different because when I was at the meeting it was the first time my mind, my body and soul were in the same place at the same time: I felt I belonged.

For the next few months, I threw myself into AA. As is suggested, I went to many meetings. My job then moved me and my family to Yorkshire, so in two ways I was able to make a new start.

I began to get an understanding of my illness and the damage I'd caused people. I started to see my son from my first marriage, who was now aged thirteen, regularly. Every weekend, I used to pick him up and he would come and stay. On the eighty-mile round trip we got to know each other better. My other three boys were now eight, six and three. I knew it was going to be a long road to become a good father, but I did my best. I made amends to my ex-wife by paying her the money I'd neglected when the marriage broke up. Most importantly, I began being a good husband to my second wife.

After twelve months in AA I started to go through its programme of recovery. I got a sponsor, a loving man called Dan. He gently guided me through the 12-Steps as outlined in the AA Big Book, just as he had been guided years before. As a result, my life gradually improved. It enabled me to understand the damage I'd caused my children, wives, parents, brothers and sisters; also, other people close to me, like former colleagues. As an active alcoholic I could see I'd been like a tornado going through people's lives. Soon I thanked God for the programme as, by doing steps 4 and 5, I saw my part in it. I was the common denominator; I was the problem and therefore I had to be the solution.

My middle son needed to see a psychologist for counselling and on one occasion I had to go, too, with my wife and children. He started asking me questions about my children when they were younger. I couldn't remember anything because in the early years of their lives I was always in blackout. I was very ashamed and broke down.

In my early years in recovery, money was tight. To clear my conscience of the financial harm I'd caused, I paid back money I'd taken or borrowed. I learned that alcohol was only a symptom of my illness: I needed to sort out the consequences it caused and reasons for my behaviour.

AA members would come to my house regularly. One woman used to babysit so I could go to meetings because my wife was working to help support the family. People took me to meetings because I couldn't afford the petrol.

The first time I saved some money, the winter was severe, so I bought my children each a new coat. It was the first time I can remember spending money on them. I was so proud. Now I know that is normal for most people, but for alcoholics of my type it was not.

It took a long time for the relationship with my wife to mend; my behaviour as a practising alcoholic, and my failed promises to stop drinking had caused deep wounds. But I was willing to go to any lengths and do what I had to do to make amends. I started to treat her as she should have been treated, with love and kindness. This was alien to me, but with time and practice I learned how to do it. I watched how other men conducted themselves and, as a result, my behaviour and our married life improved.

Two years later my employer offered me a job in Gloucester. After discussing it with my wife, we moved there. I quickly got active in AA and began taking sponsees through the 12-Steps and going to lots of meetings. As I approached my fifth year of sobriety I realised I had to address the issues around my learning difficulties, so I went to adult literacy classes. I was thirty-five years old and full of fear at going back to school to improve my very basic reading and writing skills. I found out I could get extra help by enrolling on an Open University course. My employer agreed to pay and supported me for the next few years. I eventually got a diploma in textiles. I was so proud because I'd found out I wasn't stupid. What I had was severe dyslexia.

I now applied myself more at work and got promotions, which meant travelling abroad. Today I have a senior position, an expense account, travel business class and have flown around the world on behalf of my employer several times. I am also respected, but, equally important, I now give respect, as I have learned to treat people with honesty and consideration.

As a result of putting AA's programme of recovery at the forefront of my life, I have all these blessings and many more. I have also been to five AA World Conventions in North America where there have been between 50,000 and 70,000 former alcoholics celebrating their sobriety.

As my years of sobriety went on, I was able to make amends to the rest of my family – my father in particular. I'd blamed him for the way I turned out, but the programme taught me he wasn't the problem – he did the best he could with the tools he had – I am the one responsible for my actions. So I started to visit my father regularly and spend time with him until he died years later.

As well as becoming a good son I became a good brother. So when one brother died not long ago, I was able to support his family and show them that I loved them. As well as making amends to my first wife, I thanked her new husband for being a good father to our son when I had failed to be. I also made restitution to former friends and work colleagues and, because I was sincere, not once was I told to go away and never come back. It is the AA programme that has enabled me to do all these things and to rebuild relationships.

My four boys are grown up and have turned out to be wonderful men. Over the years I have watched them mature and each has blessed my wife and me with lovely grandchildren; nine in total. Today I am able to be there for all of them in a way that I never could be for my own children because of alcohol.

My wife and I have just celebrated thirty-eight years of marriage based on love and kindness. We have taken up hill-walking in Wales and lawn bowls, and today I'm a respected member of our team. We have had holidays in amazing places such as Africa, Australia and Canada; yet when I was a drunk all I could see was one small town in Lancashire!

Today I share my recovery and help as many people as possible by passing on the AA programme, in the same way it was freely passed on to me. All my wonderful blessings are thanks to Alcoholics Anonymous and my Higher Power, which today I call God.

Chapter 25

John's Story – UK, USA and Spain

In 2005, at the age of thirty-seven, after a long, laborious process involving counselling and overseas requests for age-old original documents, I finally met my biological mother. I had begun this journey at the behest of my wife who, quite reasonably, suggested it would be a good idea to know of any hereditary health issues in my biological family that could affect our two young children. I had never considered doing it before then as I felt my adoptive parents were my real mum and dad and I felt both immense loyalty towards them and no compulsion to 'know where I had come from' or any such thing.

As it turned out, I gained a half-sister, with whom I currently have a great relationship, and some vital information about a potentially fatal genetic condition, of which I and my children are carriers. This will enable them to avoid their children being born with a killer illness through simple genetic testing in the future. However, I would be lying if I said that by the time the almost two-year process was coming to an end that was all I was hoping to find out.

Many times in Alcoholics Anonymous I have heard the expression, 'It matters little why I'm an alcoholic; the important thing is what I'm doing about it.' But I must admit that the chance to find out about my biological family and to discover whether there were problems of alcoholism or addiction (there are none in my adoptive family) had been awakening an ever-increasing curiosity in me. I had always thought there must be a genetic link to alcoholism. Time and again in AA meetings I listened to people's stories involving alcoholic parents and siblings, though, as with many things in life, there were plenty of exceptions to this rule. However, the topic is generally avoided at meetings, possibly to keep things simple for newer members who are looking for the slightest reason to convince themselves that they are not actually alcoholics and can therefore carry on drinking. When, in fact, the reality is that if we drink we could die.

Without beating about the bush, my suspicions were confirmed. I came from a family wrought with addictions of all kinds, with the usual terrible consequences. Of my two children, one has seemingly inherited this awful illness and is currently making his own slow, painful, stumbling way through the darkness of the disease towards the light of recovery; a recovery that, if the statistics are to be believed, he may never achieve.

The apparently near-impossible odds against a chronic alcoholic making a full, uninterrupted recovery are what make the stories I hear every time I attend AA meetings seem nothing short of 'an extraordinary and welcome event that is not explicable by natural or scientific laws and is therefore attributed to a divine agency' or, in a word, miraculous.

I was born at the end of the sixties in the Summer of Love and was immediately taken from my birth mother, who had been hidden away in a convent in Leeds to avoid the infamy and shame a pregnant fifteen-year-old daughter would have brought upon a family back then. Soon after, I was handed over to my adoptive parents, who did their very best for me from that moment on.

I had a relatively privileged upbringing: great holidays, a beautiful house and a good school. However, as a young boy I was awkward, shy and perpetually anxious. I was ashamed of being thin and felt generally inadequate. My father made wine and, from a young age I would be given sips, but my love affair with alcohol began on my ninth birthday in Tenerife in the Canary Islands. The setting: a cavern restaurant with a 'pay one price, drink all you want' meal deal; wine with the food and later cava (Spanish champagne) for the disco. Waiters were roaming around looking for glasses to fill, no questions of age asked. The fact a nine-year-old would remember all these details for the rest of his life strikes me now as odd and suggests that this was a truly meaningful experience. The disco was the crowning moment for me: unashamed dancing; deep feelings of joy; love and acceptance, even flirting for attention on the multi-coloured lit dance floor. I had never felt anything like it and, despite dedicating myself body and soul to recreating that wonderful night, I have hardly ever reached those heady heights again, save for some brief moments that came and went like a bee coming across the thousandth flower of the day, collecting the payload, and leaving in an instant. But the die was cast.

The next 'date' with my future lover, friend, saviour and god – booze – was at the age of thirteen. This time at a party with some of my then seventeen-year-old sister's friends. It was the first house party I had been to and I was very excited. I remember walking in through the front door, going straight to the kitchen, grabbing a bottle of some homemade alcohol and drinking it. I then vaguely recall being on a bed, vomiting, and waiting for my dad to pick me up. The next morning I awoke feeling fine, no hangover, which, I think, is what annoyed my parents more than anything. Lesson learned? Sadly not.

The boat back to Hull from Oostende was packed with travellers, including my schoolmates, coming home from a two-week school exchange in Heidelberg, Germany. I was fourteen and in the penultimate year of secondary school. Having persuaded an older student to buy me a bottle of Cinzano, I then ran around the ferry drunk and disorderly, dragging the school's name through the mud. I was stopped and taken to a dining area where I remember the headmaster saying (I always remembered what people said, but just could not respond or move when drunk in those early days) 'You are going to pay for this tomorrow morning because when you wake up you are going to feel dreadful.' Once again, no hangover and no lesson learned; though an enraged headmaster.

From that moment on, practically all my time, effort, and money was dedicated to acquiring and consuming alcohol and smoking. My dinner money, paper round and grocery delivery job paid for my habits. I left school just before my sixteenth birthday with a handful of O' levels, passed by the skin of my teeth. I believe I had issues such as ADHD or juvenile depression that would have been spotted nowadays. But instead I became a troublesome, belligerent adolescent, running away from home for days, insulting and fighting with my parents.

I left home at seventeen as the relationship with my parents had totally broken down. I had drunk more or less every day since leaving school and the need for alcohol made decisions for me, and my mental health was suffering. Age eighteen, I was treated for depression after a neighbour noticed I wasn't well and suggested going to the doctor for help, but I never gave the medication a chance because I realised it would interfere with my alcohol use.

For the next four years I was blown about by the storm of alcoholism, never taking a serious decision about my future until entering AA. I consider myself reasonably intelligent and never had trouble finding a job – my problem was keeping them. I worked my way around London and then the USA, never staying in one place longer than six months. My erratic behaviour and constant need for excessive amounts of alcohol caused me to become more and more isolated. The thought of suicide became a close companion, my deep, alcohol-induced depression just a normal part of everyday life.

The first ray of light broke through one evening in London when I was nineteen. I was overstaying my welcome on the sofa in a friend's house when, out of the blue, the girl who lived in the room downstairs came up and, along with another friend who lived there, challenged my drinking habits and suggested I may have a problem. It was far too soon for me to stop drinking, but, as we say in AA, the seed of doubt had been planted in my mind. Was I an alcoholic?

The second ray of light shone abruptly and brightly a year later, at a time when my drinking and drug-taking had become a form of self-medication; this was to satisfy the unquenchable thirst for blackouts in order to forget the pain and suffering that life seemed to bring me every single day. They also wiped away the humiliation and guilt over my previous day's behaviour. Without going into detail, suffice to say there was very little I wouldn't do to get money for alcohol and drugs and, once drunk, there was very little I didn't do! And when you take into account I was still the same shy, awkward, inadequate, anxious me underneath, the need to black out my circumstances with alcohol becomes understandable.

But back to the ray of light: it was somewhere in San Francisco, I was on all fours, crawling, drunk, and trying to hail a cab. What normal, sensible cab driver was going to stop to pick up a fare in that condition? Well, a cab did pull up. I fell inside and promptly asked the most normal of questions in that situation – 'Got anything to drink?' A few seconds later he passed back a quarter of bourbon. My favourite! Was I in Heaven? A few seconds more and he passed back a blue book, saying something like, 'Drink this tonight and read that tomorrow.' I followed the first part of his instructions to the letter and the next day, whilst scrambling around looking for something to drink in a friend's place, I came across the blue book and flicked through it out of curiosity. I couldn't handle the first half of it, which seemed strange and impossible to understand, but at the back there were stories of people's experiences with alcohol. I read them, remembering the chat from a year or so before. I don't recall what else went through my mind, but another seed of doubt had been planted. However, I still wasn't ready to stop; I just couldn't imagine life without alcohol.

So I went back to London with chronic depression, doing jobs I loathed, drinking, drugging, weeping, humiliating myself in public, fighting, lonely, continually broke, and, to make things even more fun, I had developed a religious psychosis which terrified me – I believed God despised me, the Devil hated me, and that they had got together and hatched a plan to send me to Hell. Coupled with that was a seething self-hatred.

The third and final ray of light pierced through this wretchedness a year later, back in the US in Athens, Georgia. One night in a bar I met a sweet girl who befriended me. It turned out her mother was a member of AA and she a member of Al-anon, an association for family and friends of alcoholics. She took me to meet her mother, a lovely person, who told me of her experience with alcoholism and gently suggested it might help me.

A few days later I was in a bathroom and had a razor blade at my wrist. I had weighed up my options: I could kill myself and risk going to perpetual Hell, or continue as I was. I was at the end. I chose death. Very feebly, due to the utter terror which death held for me, I began cutting at my wrist. Just then I heard loud knocks at the door and a woman burst inside with the girl whose apartment it was and grabbed me. Having spoken to me in a bar earlier that evening, she had become concerned for my welfare and followed me back to the apartment. After some hesitation she had decided to check up on me. She stayed and took care of me that night and the next day I attended my first Alcoholics Anonymous meeting. I can't remember her name and I never saw her again, but I have thanked God for her intervention every day of my sober life since.

After a week I had to go back to London. I was shaky and looked awful. Airport security spotted me, and I was checked for drugs and explosives – they didn't like the Moroccan border-security stamp in my passport – and I was given an armed escort on to the plane. This was in 1990, well before the present-day levels of airport security.

I was now homeless, broke and stone-cold sober. I contacted a friend of a friend who let me stay the night. We went out in a group and I took the decision to accept these people's generosity and drink again. That night I couldn't get drunk or high, instead I just became mentally confused and humiliated myself by going to the toilet in the wrong room. Next morning, while walking across Putney Bridge, I realised I had three options: continue drinking, kill myself, or go to Alcoholics Anonymous. I went to a meeting that evening and have not drunk or used drugs since. This was mid-August 1990.

That rain-soaked night was spent in a lift in a housing estate in Camden. The following day, I contacted a friend who let me sleep on the floorboards of his squat. Two weeks later my body gave in and I was taken to St Thomas's Hospital in South London. I was seriously underweight and after a few days of tests and unsuccessful treatment for the cause of whatever it was that was making the skin of my face fall off in a bloody, pussy goo, a doctor casually said, as if telling me it was time for tea, 'I think you have AIDS.' I didn't doubt his diagnosis, having lived in San Francisco where promiscuity, unprotected sex and love-ins were the norm.

What happened next is the most precious of the many gifts I have received during my time on this planet, one which marked the beginning of the end of my hell on earth. As I lay there contemplating my disgusting, painful demise, I calmly thought to myself, Well, if I am going to die, I want to go clean and sober.

In the space of a month since my first AA meeting something radical had changed in me. I did not enter that place wanting to stop drinking, but rather looking for a way out of the pain and suffering, neither believing I could stop nor having faith that the health and happiness I perceived in other members of AA would be possible for me to achieve. Yet, lying there, on what I thought would be my deathbed (having AIDS was still a death sentence back then) I wanted what I saw in my fellow drunks in recovery. This did not happen by mistake. I now see things more clearly and, I believe, understand how this change occurred.

At my next two meetings people were very kind and insisted on me joining them for coffee afterwards. One man was most generous and bought me a full roast meal – the first proper meal I'd had in months. Over the ensuing days people gave me their telephone numbers, called me, met up with me and took me to other meetings, and gave me a little money. In other words, they offered me unconditional love. I desperately wanted what they had; the alternative was horrific. This bought me the time I needed to come to accept that instead of being a useless, pathetic, idiotic waste of space, I was, in fact, just an alcoholic. I found a sponsor (an experienced member of AA who guides a newcomer through the twelve-step programme of recovery) started work on myself, and have never looked back.

My escape from the cesspit of alcoholism, which, according to statistics, less than 5% of chronic alcoholics achieve, has been based upon a spiritual programme of recovery, which begs the question – is it miraculous? I believe this book helps to answer this. For myself, at the time, I thought it was necessary to discover first if a divinity exists and, if so, what, who and where this God is?

I could never respond adequately to any of these questions and have stopped worrying about them. I only know that from the moment I started following a simple, spiritual way of life by helping others without seeking any recompense, other than the satisfaction of having given freely of my time, and having an open mind to ideas such as humility, self-appraisal, atonement, prayer and meditation, I have never needed to drink alcohol or take drugs which would lead me back to the unbearable suffering and despair of the past.

Chapter 26

Rachel's story – Food, Drugs and Alcohol

Born in the mid-1960s, the third and last child of a middle-to-working-class couple. Unplanned apparently, but nothing was going to stop me from entering the world, not even the contraceptive that apparently slipped.

So here I came, a girl who my parents were convinced was going to be a boy and had prenamed me David John. I was a quiet baby, happy to gurgle up at the birds in the trees from my pram, where I was often placed at the end of the garden as was the trend in those days.

Nothing remarkable or unremarkable took place. I grew up in Bristol struggling to come to terms with being the youngest of a brother and sister. My sister has bright blue eyes, an hourglass figure and blonde ringlets. Me, not so appealing, with plumpness, freckles and red wavy hair, which my mother had a thing about cutting and putting in rollers to straighten. My family was pretty dysfunctional behind closed doors. It all looked good on the outside: private schooling, and holidays to Devon three times a year, a speedboat in the double garage of a detached house. Sadly, behind the closed doors not all was as ideal as was presented to the outside world. Affairs, prescription medication dependency, alcohol, diet aids and keeping up with the Joneses all took their toll on my childhood. I retreated into books, fantasy, occult and detective thrillers to escape reality. When the rows became unbearable and the atmosphere could be cut by a knife, food became my solace, hence the inevitable bullying, teasing and ridicule that I received as I grew in weight.

The sweetness of the food, the need for comfort and nurturance ran alongside my self-loathing, guilt and shame for looking different from my peers. Add to that a bicycle accident where I lost my front teeth, so I had poor fake substitutes from the age of eight, heavy eyelids which I trained to hold up with matchsticks, and a round belly, I had a poor sense of self. School often referred to my sister two years ahead as an example: 'If your sister can achieve this, that, and the other, then you can too.' My mother often referred to daughters of friends of hers who I should aspire to be more like, comparing and contrasting my lack of educational achievement with theirs. I was indeed unworthy of any self-love or love from others – or so I believed in those days. Being teased, bullied and ridiculed at home and at school about my general appearance did nothing to help my self-esteem.

It was only a matter of time in my mid-teens when I began to smoke. This was a great substitute for food, and I managed to lose some of my childhood roundness. Add dancing into the mix, which I discovered I was pretty good at, meant I got attention from the boys, which was good enough to keep me inspired to live. Life at home was pretty volatile at times, suicide attempts from my mother, my father disappearing for days at times, alcohol and lifestyle taking their toll on their marriage.

Having discovered the opposite sex and my ability to lure them to notice me through moving my body, the time came when I had the opportunity to go on my first real diet. I had left home to attend a secretarial college in Oxford through the weeks and so was able to choose what to eat and when. I found a deeper sense of order and solution to all the feelings of loneliness, inadequacy, overwhelming fear of insecurity and vulnerability. As long as I kept to my strict food and exercise regime all would be well. I was able to handle life, being away from home, new sexual relationships, money issues, etc. at the age of 18 – as long as I kept to my diet and exercise regime. This was doomed to failure from the start. I was 8 stone 4 lbs when I began my diet as I was too fat. 5 foot 3 inches tall, size 10/12. Healthy BMI, healthy weight, curvy body.

One year later, I was one stone lighter and had begun my relationship with vodka and an older man. It was nothing for me to share my bed with three men in one night, returning to my older man friend who liked to see the hips on a woman. So, I persevered. I wanted hips, I wanted his love, and I wanted the glamour of the French restaurants and the fast cars, as well as the luxurious flats and the holidays abroad. I needed to have the hips.

By 21 I was below 6 stone, with a Body Mass Index (BMI) of 14.9. My menstruation had ceased, and I was still obsessed by my disease to be thinner, seriously believing that I was fat and not good enough for love. I was in the grips of starvation; my body and mind were frantic with the illness. I was putting my heart at risk by walking miles in extreme Australian heat every day, living off a few cups of black coffee, and one slice of meat with an apple. I had replaced alcohol at this point with a religion which banned alcohol and smoking, so in my need for love and comfort I was taken in and believed in the all-encompassing love that this particular religion offered.

However, no matter how I perfected my reading of the bible and other related writings of a metaphysical nature endorsed by the religion my eating disorder did not abate. This only encouraged my mind to think the worst of me and it was just a matter of time before I ended up in bed with a fellow 'new recruit' who had a history of drug and alcohol abuse, in and out of prison most of his adult life, but who had now found God.

Neither of us was looking at the underlying issues – we had 'put down' some of the substances, but were smothering ourselves with spiritual platitudes and promises of the religion which comforted us but did not address our disease.

So, a few years went by and I had become a single mum of one child – my ex-husband in prison yet again, and me back on the wine, cigarettes and now bulimic and still searching for a meaningful existence, in some right places (I taught yoga and was a complementary therapist), but mainly in all the wrong places. (The religion had long been discarded.)

And so it went on, and on, and on. It was the norm. It was my 'banality of evil'.

It was tedious, boring, lonely, exhausting, futile, depressing, full of self-loathing and self-grandiosity, the paradox of living within a mind full of hypocrisy and perfectionism. A mind desperate to be 'right' and yet desperate to be free at the same time. A mind that could not function healthily on fresh air, caffeine, tobacco and wine with little else feeding it. It did not matter how many self-help books I read or different therapies I received, being underweight, undernourished and poisoning myself with alcohol and tobacco did not leave my mind able to make rational decisions.

The gift of desperation came upon me when I was 38 years of age. I knew I was beaten by my eating disorder, having accepted it as par for the course, and the alcohol was getting me into all sorts of situations and behaving in diabolical ways – all of which I swore that I would never do.

I had read about Alcoholics Anonymous in my self-help books, and so, with trepidation ringing in my head, I rang their helpline. I was strongly advised to take myself to a meeting as soon as possible and so I did.

There began my journey of self-discovery and recovery. I needed to let go of my addiction to alcohol to enable me to get help with my eating disorder. AA was the only place that had worked with me to begin that journey. I sat in my first meeting and identified with the speaker, her words echoing into the desperation of my heart, offering me the first glimmer of hope that I'd had for many years.

I got the sponsor, I did the steps, I took service positions, and went to many meetings. I stopped drinking and I behaved differently in so many ways, but my eating disorder got louder. It began to take me by the throat again and had me twisted within its grasp, hurtling me internally towards a steaming cauldron of destruction and despair. Outwardly I looked good, my weight was decent, though still low, I had highlights in my hair, and I dressed becomingly. Walking upright and with poise due to the years of yoga, I was convincing myself and others in the fellowship that I was 'all right'.

Eventually I crumbled. I drank; I hated myself, and I drank more. For six long months I continued to convince myself that I was in control. I drank longer and harder than ever before, with greater consequences, car smashes, bedmates who I knew little about, isolation and loneliness like nothing I had ever experienced. My life was leaving me, and my daughter was crying out for me.

I surrendered – finally. I gave up the control, the self-enforced slavery to the bottle and to the self-image that I had created. I had to release all power to find recovery. Open, vulnerable, broken and destroyed, I began the best phase of my life. I knew I had to stay stopped from alcohol in order to give myself a chance of life and to give myself the opportunity to learn how to relate to myself and to food.

It has been tough and very rewarding. The twelve steps and the recovery programme have been invaluable in enabling me to stop drinking alcohol and to manage some of my mental health issues. I sought outside help for my eating disorder as I found that Overeaters Anonymous was not right for me. I wanted to trust myself, to have a good relationship with myself and with the food that I was putting into my body.

I have been a healthy, stable weight for twelve years now and I know when I am emotionally out of kilter as my food will be the first to go. My father died about four years ago, suddenly. I found him, tried to resuscitate him, but it was too late. Inevitably, due to the emotional upset surrounding all of this, my instinct was to stop eating, a natural grief reaction. However, as I know how quickly my mind could grab that and run with it as a solution to all my emotional problems, I deliberately and consciously made sure that I had regular, if only small, meals.

I know how important it is to stay on top of my eating disorder as I have to eat in order to maintain a level of health in both my body and my mind. Unlike alcohol, which I can now choose to stay away from one day at a time, I do need to food in my life. Therefore, it is imperative that I maintain a healthy mental attitude towards myself and towards life. I have to work on my relationship with myself, accepting and loving myself for who I am on a daily basis, learning healthy boundaries and making wise decisions on lifestyle choices which endorse me rather than destroy me. Compassion is key to my life today, towards myself and to others.

Without the AA programme I would not have found the courage to stop drinking. Without the AA programme I would still be in the cycle of anorexia/bulimia while getting superficial energy from caffeine and alcohol. I thank goodness that there is such a programme of recovery out there as I now can have peace of mind as well as a healthy body. I have healthy relationships and friends that I never had before. I genuinely like myself and respect the natural limitations that my body has. So today I am a grateful alcoholic and the AA's 12-Step programme began my journey to life.

Chapter 27

A psychotherapists experience of 12 step programmes

The clinical world has a lot to thank AA for, and vice versa. It is no accident that over 90% of private treatment facilities worldwide are based on the Twelve Step method. Several million recovering members of AA worldwide are testament to the fact that the AA programme works. Add to these millions of sufferers from other addictive processes who are recovering in Twelve Step-based fellowships such as Narcotics Anonymous (NA), Over Eaters Anonymous (OA), Gamblers Anonymous (GA), Anorexics and Bulimics Anonymous (ABA), Co-dependency Anonymous (CODA), Sex Addicts (SAA), Sex and Love Addicts (SLA), Debtors Anonymous (DA). Plus, Al-Anon, Nar-Anon and Family's Anonymous, the fellowships for those family members of alcoholics and addicts who have had their mental health seriously damaged by living with or loving the addict in their lives.

Recovery from addiction is hugely enhanced by the support of close family and friends, and their understanding of addiction as an illness rather than a moral weakness. So, to summarize, there are Twelve Step fellowships that cover recovery every manifestation of that many-headed-monster known as Addiction. And they are entirely free!

It is also true that many addictions counsellors are recovering addicts or alcoholics themselves. On the basis that it takes one to really know one, a highly trained and qualified counsellor in good personal recovery makes an ideal recruit for any inpatient or outpatient treatment centre specialising in addiction. And since the recommended aftercare programme of all these treatment facilities is regular attendance at fellowship meetings, we start to see that the most effective clinically based treatment facilities are totally dependent on the Twelve Step fellowships for their treatment mode, for their staff, and for post treatment aftercare.

So why do the Twelve Step fellowships have much to thank the clinicians for? For the answer to this question, we must first look at the negatives that the Twelve Step fellowships present to many active alcoholics and addicts seeking recovery. AA and NA are frequently perceived as religions with too much emphasis on a religious God. While this perception is totally inaccurate, and while the welcome that a newcomer receives when he attends his/her first meeting is always friendly and non-judgemental, it is a fact that this negative perception puts off large numbers of alcoholics and addicts from investigating further. In fact, the fellowships are not allied with any religion, but founded and practiced on spiritual lines. But spiritual is also an often, misunderstood word that can have a negative impact in the increasingly secular world we live in. If the newcomer to AA gets over his/her initial prejudices in the first few weeks of attendance at meetings, he or she will discover that they are free to choose any power greater than themselves as long as it's not them!

Without realising it, all using addicts and practicing alcoholics have played God in their own lives – much to the disadvantage of themselves and their families.

The evidence of the non-religious, non-denominational nature of the Twelve Step programme lies in the composition of every AA/NA meeting. Here men and women of all faiths and all ethnic origins, including atheists and religious sceptics, band together joyously, reaching out to each other with compassion. This is the beating heart of all Twelve Step fellowship meetings.

The clinical approach to the treatment of addiction provides a much easier and more familiar entry to the Twelve Step world. For a start, it is so much easier for a frightened and desperate using alcoholic to talk privately and in confidence to a doctor-like therapist in a quiet room than to go to his first AA meeting full of strangers. For many this is too daunting a prospect. The idea that he/she feels expected to talk about themselves in front of a crowd of strangers is truly daunting. Also, the therapist's client has almost certainly been treated as a bad person who needs to become good by his family and friends. Suddenly, after years of abuse and pain, he or she finds themselves dealing with someone who is understanding and non-judgemental, who doesn't shout at them, and who explains that he or she is not a bad person but is in fact a very ill person who needs to get well. They have a disease that can be healed. In this way the therapist starts to build trust between himself and his client, and the process of lighting the flame of hope that he or she can recover begins.

Soon the therapist is able to suggest that inpatient or outpatient treatment would be the best option for the client. If the client agrees, he or she finds themselves in another clinical environment – not unlike a comfortable private hospital, amongst a small group of fellow patients whom he/she quickly identifies with and makes new friends. He or she is treated with respect and over the next weeks or months, they receive a university degree type education in all things' addiction. Most important of all they become fully prepared for the main event – their entry into the equally non-judgmental and loving environment of the Twelve Step programme.

But private treatment centres are expensive, and addictions counsellors see plenty of new clients who cannot afford the cost. Many deal with this situation by insisting that their client go to three or four appropriate Twelve Step fellowship meetings per week, in addition to regular therapy sessions. The experienced therapist needs to remember that he/she is only a stepping stone on a client's journey into recovery.

I have been an addiction-based psychotherapist for twenty five years and in my personal recovery for thirty seven years. I believe that the combination of trained therapists specialising in addiction treatment, working in close harness with the Twelve Step programme, has provided the world with the most comprehensive and effective solution to the huge problem and cost to society of the illness of addiction.

The number of addicts and alcoholics who join Twelve Step fellowships via professional therapy and treatment centres is increasing year by year. My estimate is that in many places 40% of AA and NA members have been introduced to the Twelve Step fellowships via clinicians and/or treatment centres. I believe that this percentage is much higher in current newcomers to the programme. But there is still much work to be done to enable more addicts and alcoholics to find recovery. Membership of Twelve Step fellowships is free but private therapy and treatment is expensive.

Unfortunately, there is a huge gap between the quality of private treatment and that which is available generally from the state. If governments were to accept that the money they currently spend on a variety of addiction treatment modes could be spent on establishing the latest Twelve Step based models – free at the point of delivery - millions more could be healed. Then the huge cost to nations would decline dramatically, many prisoners would cease to reoffend, the load on our hospitals would be greatly eased, and the mental health of the people would be hugely improved.

Hopefully, the recovery stories relating to many different addictions and emotional issues in this book will be the catalyst to make these happen.

Johnny C-R

Chapter 28

Summary

In the four years it took to write this book, approximately 11 million people died from alcoholism or drug addiction, with less than 10% given the opportunity to recover. This means that because of the world's drug laws and ineffective treatment of addiction, millions died, families and society suffered, without it being made clear there is a freely available solution which could have saved many of their lives and much suffering.

As more and more truths about the disease of addiction unfold, the writers realised the stigma of being an alcoholic or drug addict is historic and a major obstacle to recovery. There is now compelling evidence which proves this was as a direct result of prohibition in the 1920s and using the slogan 'the war on drugs' from the 1970s onwards.

This led to three equally bad revelations:

1. These politically inspired, badly judged regimes had created birthplaces for criminals. Formerly innocent, mostly young, people were sentenced to prison for drug-related offences, place which are nurseries for hardened lawbreakers of the most serious crimes, including radicalisation into terrorism.

2. Pharmaceutical firms have been exposed for giving misinformation to doctors to prescribe their drugs, many of which are as addictive and dangerous as so-called hard drugs.

3. Because of the enormity of the multi-billion-dollar global addictive prescription drugs market, created by politicians and Big Pharma, drug cartels and mafias have boarded this money-spinning, deadly bandwagon.

Just as extraordinary as politicians and the pharmaceutical industry's denial that they are the cause of many of the world's drug problems, is that the evidence for these facts is most obvious in the United States of America. Each of these regimes was hatched there, but the lessons that should have been learned from their knock-on effects have been ignored; so the corrections that are essential have not been made.

First fact. Alcohol prohibition in a twelve-year period led to social mayhem and bloodshed on a colossal scale.

Second fact. Prescription painkiller addiction to opiates has driven thousands of users to heroin addiction.

The overall effect is that America's blinkered and hypocritical attitude to addiction and its drug laws have been directly responsible for turning innocent people into hardened criminals. As soon as a doctor becomes aware that someone is addicted to opiates, they have to stop prescribing them. The consequence is, the easiest place the now desperate addict can go to get their fix is the heroin dealer. And because heroin possession or use gives them a criminal record, the addict cannot get a job; so they rob, steal, burgle or prostitute themselves to feed their habit, ending up in prison.

The result is many times more crime, and criminals are created out of ordinary people. A scenario which is fact in almost every country in the world.

The writers' stories and millions of other addicts' experience, upon which *Millions of Miracles* is based, exposes these issues and by doing so automatically identifies a lot of the solution. The book's true stories do this by clearly identifying the political and financial causes and how there is a programme of recovery available for all forms of addiction. This works whenever an addict of any type applies its principles.

It also makes clear that far too often the AA and NA programmes that are needed are not made available to those who suffer because the medical profession, far too often lacks the right direction and understanding regarding the disease of addiction. This is because it and the public have been misled by vote-chasing politicians, who use fear as their weapon, and the greed of pharmaceutical companies, who tell them their products and harm reduction are the best way to tackle addiction. The facts prove categorically this is not the case.

This has led to a form of stigmatisation that makes the problem many times worse. It has meant alcoholics and drug addicts are treated as mentally deficient, pathetic, weak-willed, and if they become criminals, they are tagged with this as well. Society then brands them as undesirables and the terrible stigma of being a drug addict is complete.

When the facts are known it becomes clear, the laws and policies relating to drug addicts and alcoholics camouflaged the fact they caused a form of racism. They are sick people who need help, and as the help they need to recover is available, every one of them should be offered the chance to have it.

This situation has been brought about by politicians who played politics with drugs and addiction, while the biggest paymasters of America's political lobbying system, pharmaceutical firms, use them as puppets as they pull the strings. This allows the pharmaceutical firms to come up with more and more addictive drug substitutes, all of which prevent addicts from dealing with their underlying problems. The addicts stay hooked and Big Pharma reaps the rewards. Which is why drug problems today are as bad as they have ever been. This will not change unless the underlying political and pharmaceutical industry's causes are addressed.

The result is that today, neither politicians and legal addictive prescription drug makers will admit they are wrong for fear of public anger and huge financial repercussions. But as there is overwhelming factual evidence that prohibition and the war on drugs have failed, that addiction is a disease, and the only known solution is permanent total abstinence, the time has come for the medical profession and public to demand these wrongs are righted.

As with other forms of racism and terrible wrongs, such as apartheid, the criminalising of homosexuality, to women before they got the vote, the British occupation of India, justice eventually prevailed and each of these barbaric issues was rectified. So must it be with drugs and addiction.

The current drug laws and prevailing attitudes are equally inhumane and racist. It is time for the erroneous facts to be recognised, for it is no more an addict's fault they have an allergy to a drug than it is for your son or daughter, brother or sister, mother or father to have diabetes, coronary heart disease, Ebola, Parkinson's or Alzheimer's diseases, to be black, or gay. (In fact, if a pregnant woman is a practising illegal drug addict, her baby will be born with the same addiction, and it cannot be right it would be tagged a criminal.)

This means the United Nations must:

(a)   recommend that the programmes used by the millions of recovered addicts worldwide are offered in _every_ instance to anyone suffering the disease of addiction.

(b)   endorse unequivocally the success decriminalisation of drug laws has had in the countries and US states that have done so.

(c)   recommend without reservation decriminalisation or legalisation be applied in every country in the world.

(d)   remove from its manifesto the ability of single countries to veto such a decision as Russia did in April 2016 for purely self-interests.

Aside from pharmaceutical firms, the main beneficiaries of the past and present regimes of prohibition and the war on drugs are the cartels and mafia groups, to whom these policies gave birth. As the contraband they market has grown into a multi-billion-dollar industry run by the most disreputable criminals, whose products attract innocent people, and once addicted become criminals themselves, the putting in place of such policies should be a no-brainer.

The drug problems current laws were meant to control could only get hundreds of times worse and they did, to the point where only a complete reversal of policies and attitudes can rectify the situation. This naively created international graveyard has destroyed as many lives and caused as much harm to society as any other of man's mindless blunders since we arrived on the planet. But until recent years, reality has been hidden from the public by political spin and fear-driven politics. Unfortunately, this worked because the offences drug addicts commit to feed their habit often lead to some of the most serious crimes: terrorist attacks such as those in Barcelona, Paris, London, Brussels, Madrid, Casablanca and Marrakesh, murder, gang wars, gunfights, burglary, theft, extortion, rape and prostitution, which tarnished their reputations and politicians used this to make their case.

These facts have led to prisons and criminal courts being more than 60% taken up by drug-influenced crime. And because of the historical villainous stigma associated with drugs, alcohol, prostitution and gambling, the courts' officers, prison wardens, governors, probation officers and police treat them as criminals because they have never been made aware of the reality; this is racism.

The cost of keeping a criminal in prison is approximately $100 a day. As America has the highest number of inmates in the world – 2.2 million, including probation and parole, it is $7 million – the total annual cost is a staggering $80 billion. (US Bureau of Justice Statistics) Presumably, similar statistics apply elsewhere as more or less the same laws and policies apply.

According to the International Narcotics Control Board (INCB), prescription drugs have moved up to second on the list of the most abused and trafficked types of drugs in the world. This board, established by the United Nations, reports that demand for painkillers, sedatives, stimulants and tranquillisers is developing rapidly, while the global consumption of heroin and cocaine has decreased.

Similar crime and drug use statistics apply all over the world. In the United Kingdom in June 2016 British MPs made the following statement:

'The criminal justice system in England and Wales is failing victims and witnesses and close to breaking point'. The Public Accounts Committee (PAC) said the system was 'bedevilled by long-standing poor performance, including delays and inefficiencies'.

The report found that about two-thirds of trials in crown courts were delayed or did not go ahead at all and there was a backlog of 51,830 cases awaiting a hearing as of September the previous year, with an average 134-day wait between cases leaving magistrates' courts and the start of crown court proceedings.

By applying the 60% factor explained above, in one simple move decriminalisation would decimate these figures; plus, there would be massive financial savings and many societal benefits.

The overall result is that we live in a world which believes that 10% of its population are at best second-class, at worst hardened criminals. Whereas they are not. They are human beings the same as the other 90% and need to have the opportunity for their disease to be treated in the same way as the three and a half million who have recovered.

On top of the crime figures are the costs of accidents, domestic violence, family breakdowns, fire and health issues which fill our hospitals and plague society.

The World Health Organisation says that 'Psychoactive substance use poses a significant threat to the health, social and economic fabric of families, communities and nations. The extent of worldwide psychoactive substance use is estimated at 2 billion alcohol users, 1.3 billion smokers and 185 million drug users.'

Yet still the United Nations allows single members to veto changes to drug laws that, if implemented, would help rectify the global problems. At the UN General Assembly Special Session on Drugs (UNGASS) in New York in April 2016, a delegation from Russia – which houses some of the most notorious drug mafias in the world – caused this to happen. But for addicts who live in Russia, which has one of the worst opiate addiction problems in the world – it borders Afghanistan, which grows 90% of the world's heroin – this is worse than Russian roulette. While they and the other major mafia units and cartels make mountains of money because of the world's drug laws – the USA, Mexico, Japan, Italy, Netherlands and Israel – laugh as they fill their substantial money-laundering coffers with billions in banknotes in exchange for bouquets of poppies and coca leaves.

Plus, the United Nations allows its members to defy all humanitarian logic. Some countries apply the death penalty to its drug offenders, while others, for committing exactly the same offence, don't even send their offenders to prison; they apply small fines or give a caution.

In other words, the world's drug laws, prohibition, and the 'war on drugs' has done no good whatsoever and still causes massive social and financial problems.

Due to these absurdities, the WHO needs to make categorically clear, by exposing all the evidence, that current American and UN policies are the backbone of the world's gargantuan drug problem. This will pave the way for governments, lawmakers, pharmaceutical, alcohol, tobacco and gambling firms, followed by the medical profession, to change the current policies. As these policies cause drug-related harm to society, families and financially; and prevent millions of addicts from recovering.

These fact-based revelations would also help remove the tarnished reputations attached to alcoholism and illegal drug addiction which are major obstacles to recovery, put pressure on politicians to change the world's hypocritical drug laws, and lead the police, media and public to having their deep-rooted erroneous views about drugs and addiction corrected. The knock-on effect could only be positive and in a very short time the repercussions would filter into society; lives would be saved, and crimes, accidents and austerity measures cut.

From every angle it is time to change.

Chapter 29

Solution

Current international drug control policies have not decreased consumption, curbed the planting of crops destined for the illicit market, or curtailed the expanding drug trade. Instead, they have marginalised drug users, who are pushed out of reach of treatment programmes, repressed farmers, who may have no other means of survival, and overwhelmed criminal justice systems. In fact, such policies have targeted users and small-scale traffickers, while the large-scale criminal organisations and mafias have remained unrestrained.

The Transnational Institute was founded in 1974 as the international programme of the US based Institute for Policy Studies. Its mission has been entwined with the history of global social movements and their struggle for economic, social and environmental justice. Its Drug Law Reform Project promotes more effective and humane drug policies through analysis of existing drug control policies and by promoting dialogue among key decision makers. The project hopes to stimulate reforms by pointing out good practices and lessons learned.

Its comment on the outcome of the UN Commission on Narcotic Drugs in April 2016 was *'a disappointing compromise, based on a non-inclusive process and one that fails to reflect the fractured global consensus on drug policy'.*

Decriminalisation

The success of cannabis decriminalisation in the countries that have made it law speaks for itself.

1. It frees billions of dollars now used to prosecute users to rehabilitate addicts.
2. Provides billions in tax revenue.
3. Frees a substantial amount of law-enforcement resources which can be used to prevent more serious crimes.
4. Frees substantial amounts of prison resources.
5. Reduces the income, therefore the number and strength of street gangs and organised crime who grow, import, process and sell drugs.

Opponents argue that cannabis on the street today has a higher per cent of THC, the psychoactive part of cannabis, and decriminalisation will lead to more usage, increased crime, and abuse of more dangerous illicit drugs.

The facts prove these sceptics 100% wrong.

Portugal

In 1997 about 45% of reported AIDS cases were among intravenous users. By 1999 nearly 1% of the Portuguese population was addicted to heroin and drug-related AIDS deaths were the highest in the European Union.

In the year 2000 the decriminalisation of drugs was being discussed in Portugal's parliament and a year later the policy was changed. As a direct consequence blood-borne, sexually transmitted diseases and drug overdoses have dramatically decreased. Targeting drug use became an effective HIV-prevention measure. It was decided to treat the possession and use of drugs as a public health issue, so instead of a criminal record and/or a prison sentence, addicts would get a fine and/or a referral (that wasn't compulsory) to a treatment programme. As a result, money saved from taking individuals through the criminal justice system started being spent on rehabilitation and get-back-to-work schemes.

In the last fourteen years, drug use has diminished among the fifteen-to-twenty-four-year age group. There has also been a decline in the percentage of the population who have ever used a drug and then continued to do so. Drug-induced deaths decreased steeply and, at present, Portugal has three overdoses per million citizens, compared to the EU average of 17.3! HIV infection has steadily reduced and has become a more manageable problem. There has been a similar downward trend for cases of hepatitis B and C. This policy was complemented by allocating resources to the drugs field, expanding and improving prevention, treatment, harm reduction and social reintegration.

AA and NA are available in Portuguese.

USA

Since prohibition began in 1920, drug use has increased in all categories. The Reagan, Nixon and Bush administration's 'War on Drugs' policy has proved to be a disaster. Today US prisons have more inmates than any other country in the world, half of whom are there for drug-related offences.

A recent review of its failed policies is now giving way to more relaxed drug laws. Most states are considering rehabilitation as opposed to incarceration for drug users. More than half of US States and the District of Columbia have made the use of marijuana legal for medical use. Many Americans have come to believe that all drugs should be legalised and the money now being spent to incarcerate drug users should be redirected to rehabilitation and drug education.

Another problem in the US is the influence in Congress of the drug testing industry. It is worth $4 billion a year and growing, and given its status, its voice gets heard, a voice that is unlikely to support legalisation.

In 2012, **Washington and Colorado** became the first two US states to approve ending marijuana prohibition and legally regulating its production, distribution, and sales. '... prohibition has been a costly failure, to individuals, communities and the entire country.' Tamar Todd, US Drug Policy Alliance.

Washington DC

After eighteen months the following results were reported:

- Minor marijuana offences down 98% for adults 21 years and older. All categories of marijuana law violations down 63% and marijuana-related convictions down 81%.
- The state saves millions of dollars in law enforcement previously used to enforce marijuana laws.
- Violent crime decreased and other crime rates remain stable.
- Washington collects over $80 million in marijuana tax revenues. These revenues are used to fund substance abuse prevention and treatment programmes, drug education, community health care, academic research, and to evaluate the effects of legalisation in the state.
- The number of traffic fatalities remains stable.
- Youth marijuana use did not increase.
- Washington voters continue to support legalisation. 56% continue to approve the state's marijuana law while only 37% oppose, a decrease of 7 points since the election of 2012. 77% believe the law has had either a positive impact or no effect on their lives.

Colorado

The US Drug Policy Alliance issued this report on marijuana legalisation in Colorado after one year of retail sales and two years of decriminalisation.

'Since the first retail stores opened on January 1st, 2014, the state has benefitted from a decrease in crime rates, a decrease in traffic fatalities, an increase in tax revenue and an increase in jobs. Marijuana arrests and judicial savings, according to data from the Colorado Court System, have dropped around 80% since 2010. Given that such arrests cost $300 each to adjudicate, it can be inferred that the state is saving millions in adjudicatory costs for possession cases alone. Over the same period, arrests for cultivating and distributing marijuana have also dropped by more than 90%. Add to this decreases in violent crime rates released by the city of Denver, plus, burglaries fell by 9.5% and overall property crime by 8.9%.'

Along with legalisation, Colorado voters approved a 15% excise tax on wholesale marijuana sales that is only to be used for school construction. In total this brought in $135 million in new revenue in 2015, so $20.25 million goes to schools. There was also a decrease in traffic fatalities in 2014, according to data released by the Colorado Department of Transportation, challenging claims that the legalisation of marijuana would lead to an increase.

If the figures for Washington and Colorado were replicated in all fifty American states, the positive effects would be massive.

The USA has an estimated 20 million drug addicts. Currently there are 23,000 Narcotics Anonymous meetings a week spread across the country, serving less than one million. If America promoted NA's proven programme as its primary treatment for recovery from drug addiction, the results would, from every angle, all be positive.

The US National Council on Alcoholism and Drug Dependence, (NCADD) says alcohol is the most commonly used addictive substance in the United States: 17.6 million people, one in every 12 adults, suffer from alcohol abuse or dependence, along with several million more who engage in risky binge-drinking patterns that could lead to alcohol problems. More than half of all adults have a family history of alcoholism or problem drinking, and more than 7 million children live in a household where at least one parent is dependent on or has abused alcohol. 88,000 deaths are annually attributed to excessive alcohol abuse and a large percentage of hospitals and prisons are inundated with sick offenders, whose circumstances directly relate to alcohol consumption.

Yet alcohol, known to be one of the most lethal drugs, is legal. If AA's programme of recovery is proposed by America's medical profession in every instance of alcoholism, the horrendous results caused by its abuse would be drastically reduced.

AA and NA are available in English and every other language spoken in America.

Canada

At the same UNGASS conference on drugs the Canadian government announced that it would introduce legislation in 2017 to decriminalise and legalise the sale of marijuana, making Canada the first G7 country to permit widespread use of the substance.

AA and NA are available in English and French.

Uruguay

In December 2013, Uruguay became the first country in the world to completely legalise marijuana on a nationwide level. It is therefore too soon to know if it has been successful; however, there are no signs that it has not.

AA and NA are available in Spanish.

Netherlands

Drug policy in the Netherlands aims 'to reduce the demand for drugs, the supply of drugs and the risks to drug users, their immediate surroundings and society.'

The Dutch recognise that it is impossible to prevent people from using addictive drugs, because that would include alcohol and many prescription medications. Coffee shops are therefore allowed to sell small amounts of 'soft' drugs such as marijuana. This approach meant that authorities could focus on criminals, who profit from so-called 'hard' drugs.

The result is that rates of marijuana use are equivalent to, or lower than, those of nearby countries (which do not have such coffee shops), and are substantially lower than those of the USA.

Annually, the coffee shops generate an estimated 400 million euros in tax – money that would otherwise have accrued to criminal profiteers – that is used to help the Dutch community.

AA and NA are available in Dutch.

Switzerland

The Swiss policy on drugs comprises four elements: prevention, therapy, harm reduction and law enforcement. The concept of a fourfold approach to the reduction of drug-related problems was developed in the early 1990s, and now forms the principle national drug policy. As mandated by law, the Swiss Federal Office of Public Health (SFOPH) endeavours to reduce drug-related problems by being active in the following areas:

- Coordination of cooperation between federal, regional and local authorities
- primary and secondary prevention
- treatment (abstinence-based, substitution, prescription)
- harm reduction
- information and documentation
- training of professional staff
- research
- quality assurance

Although these are their federal policies, Switzerland's former president, Ruth Dreifuss, who is a member of the Global Commission on Drug Policy, has made clear her view that regulation by countries and states would take away the possibility for making big money from drug trafficking, therefore legal regulation is the way forward.

Today this view is shared by many of the world's political, business, religious and philosophical leaders and continues to gather pace.

AA and NA are available in German, French and Italian.

Iran

Due to its 1,900 km border with Afghanistan, the Islamic State of Iran probably has the worst opiate problem of any country in the world. It is estimated that 4 million of its 70 million people are addicts. This is caused partly because it lies in the middle of the drug-trafficking route from Afghanistan to Turkey and Europe, causing an estimated 140 tons of heroin to enter it annually.

Overdose in Iran is the second leading cause of death after traffic accidents, many of which are caused by drivers under the influence of opiates. Half the prison population of over 220,000 are drug traffickers or addicts. Sadly, Iran's lack of understanding of addiction means its laws sanction more executions per capita than any other country in the world, and over half those executed are drug traffickers. But the drug problem there being so vast and its thinking backward, it exposes the futility of its draconian measures, making it obvious that a major change of policy is essential to remedy the situation.

In 1990 two brothers started the first meeting of Narcotics Anonymous in Iran. Today there are more than 500,000 members spread all over the country and more than 25,000 NA meetings a week. In 2012 a local sports centre hosted an NA World Services Convention which had 24,000 former Iranian drug addicts attending. If the NA approach was adopted by the Iranian Government as its primary source of recovery from drug addiction, these statistics would reach all four million sufferers.

NA is available in Farsi.

France

French love of anti-depressants, sleeping pills and prescription narcotics has reached new heights. A study by France's National Drug Safety Agency (ANSM) found that 32% – almost 1 in 3 – French people used some form of psychotic medication in 2013, either on a regular or an occasional basis. This is in addition to having one of Europe's highest rates of alcoholism and substantial problems with illegal drug addiction.

AA and NA are available in French.

Estonia

Estonia is famous for three reasons: it has the highest number of drug deaths per capita in Europe; the highest for alcohol in the world, and it has Europe's healthiest economy.

The reason for the first is fentanyl, a high potency, synthetic opioid with a rapid onset and short active life. It is nicknamed China white, Persian white or Afghan, but these pseudonyms for 'killer drug' hide the dangers of taking this innocent-looking powder. It is produced in clandestine labs across the border in Russia, where mafia-influenced pharmacists began making it during a heroin shortage in 2002. Today it is the drug of choice for Estonia's multitude of addicts, with its scientists saying it is more than 100 times stronger than the heroin it replaced.

It seems astonishing, therefore, that it was Russia's veto at the United Nations General Assembly Special Session on Drugs (UNGASS) in April 2016 that prevented the desperately needed changes to the world's drug laws being made. (Astonishing, unless Russia's mafia have direct financial links to the highest levels of its government and the KGB.)

So, while Estonian addicts die like lemmings (murdered?) Russia's mafia continues to make billions of rubles.

AA and NA are available in Estonian.

Russia

Alcohol-related deaths per capita in Russia make it the fourth highest in the world, and for drugs they are ranked sixth.

According to *The Lancet*, it has the largest population of injecting drug users (IDUs) in the world, an estimated 1·8 million people. More than a third have HIV, and in some regions the proportion is about three-quarters of the population. An estimated 90% of their IDUs have hepatitis C, and most are drug dependent. It is estimated their drug addicts spend 4.5 billion rubles ($70 million) on drugs every day; 1.5 trillion ($23.5 billion) a year: ironically this is comparable to its defensc budget!

Approximately 30% of all deaths in Russia are attributable to alcohol, says the WHO. This is from alcohol poisoning, cirrhosis, accidents, murder and suicide.

The result? Russians live some of the shortest lives of any of the big economies: life expectancy for a Russian man is roughly 65 years, compared to 76 years in the US and 74 for Europe.

So why would Russia veto changes to the world's drug laws that are known to work when their statistics are so awful?

The answer can only be money and internal corruption.

AA and NA are available in Russian and other dialects.

Philippines

Rodrigo Duterte was elected president of the Philippines in May 2016, on promises to eradicate drugs, crime and corruption in the country. Duterte – also known as 'The Punisher' – even urged Filipino citizens to shoot and kill drug dealers themselves.
'Please feel free to call us, the police, or do it yourself if you have the gun – you have my support,' Duterte said, referring to drug dealers who show violent resistance. 'You can kill him. Shoot him and I'll give you a medal.'
Since his inauguration, thousands of suspected dealers and users have been killed.

Mexico

Over the course of the war in Afghanistan, the number of civilian deaths has been 26,000 since it began in 2001. In Iraq, conservative tallies place the number of civilians killed at 160,000 since the US invasion in 2003.

But as US involvement in each nation has dropped off in recent years, killings much closer to home, in Mexico, have outpaced the number of civilian deaths in Afghanistan and Iraq combined.

The Mexican government has released data showing that, between 2007 and 2014, a period that accounts for some of the bloodiest years of the nation's war against the drug cartels, more than 164,000 people were victims of homicide. Nearly 20,000 died last year alone, a decrease from 27,000 killed at the peak of fighting in 2011.

****

Based on the ever-growing evidence and support for decriminalisation, the rest of the world may well follow the example of Canada. And when the next G7 country – the United States, France, Germany, Italy, Japan or United Kingdom – follows suit, what began as a desperate attempt to stem its drug and HIV problem in Portugal in 2001 will promote one of the most successful advances in the treatment of a killer disease and destroyer of societies in human history since Alexander Fleming won the Nobel Prize for penicillin in 1945.

But let us hope that change comes sooner rather than later, as every minute of every hour, of every day, the costs to society, families and individuals grows higher and higher.

The situation needs the United Nations and World Health Organisation to act together and expose the truth as soon as possible, even if it means changing the UN's veto procedure to stop one country being able to block recovery from this worldwide epidemic for selfish reasons.

1. All drugs must be treated equally, decriminalised and legalised.

2. The Alcoholics Anonymous, Narcotics Anonymous programmes and every other 12-Step fellowship must be made available to every alcoholic, drug addict and person in the world that needs them.

Directory of 12-Step Programmes

Many addiction and behavioural recovery programmes have been born from Alcoholics Anonymous's, each adapted to address a specific problem from a wide range of substance and/or dependency abuse issues. Every one of these self-help fellowships employs the same 12-Step principles for recovery.

Alcoholics Anonymous and Narcotics Anonymous programmes of recovery and worldwide success are described in detail in previous chapters.

To make contact with **AA** in one of the 175 countries where it is established, go to the local AA website. Alternatively go to **http://www.aa.org/**

NA is also established worldwide. For information, contacts, or meetings go to **http:// www.na.org/**

Demographic preferences related to the addict's drug of choice has led to the creation of other non-profit self-help 12-Step fellowships such as:

Cocaine Anonymous (CA) dealing with cocaine and crack addiction. **https://www.ca.org/**

Crystal Meth Anonymous (CMA) is a relatively new twelve-step programme for people who are addicted to crystal meth. Links provide support for family and friends as well. **http://www.crystalmeth.org/**

Heroin Anonymous (HA) Heroin Anonymous is a non-profit fellowship of men and women who have found a solution to heroin addiction. HA is a fellowship of complete abstinence from all drugs and alcohol. They are recovered heroin addicts who meet regularly to help each other stay sober. The only requirement for membership is a desire to stop suffering from heroin addiction. There are no dues or fees for HA membership. HA is not allied with any sect, denomination, politics, organisation or institution; does not wish to engage in any controversy and neither endorses nor opposes any causes. Their primary purpose is to stay sober and help other heroin addicts to achieve sobriety. **https://heroinanonymous.org/**

Marijuana Anonymous (MA) is a fellowship of people who share their experience, strength and hope with each other that they may solve their common problem and help others to recover from marijuana addiction https://www.**marijuana-anonymous**.org/

Nicotine Anonymous (NicA) is a fellowship of men and women who help each other live nicotine-free lives. They welcome all those seeking freedom from nicotine addiction, including those using cessation programmes and nicotine withdrawal aids. The primary purpose of Nicotine Anonymous is to help all those who would like to cease using tobacco and nicotine products in any form. The fellowship offers group support and recovery, using the 12-Steps as adapted from Alcoholics Anonymous to achieve abstinence from nicotine **https://www.nicotine-anonymous.org/**

Pills Anonymous (PA) is a fellowship of recovering pill addicts – prescription drugs - throughout the world who share their experience, strength and hope as to how they stopped using pills. **http://pillsanonymous.org/**

Behavioural addictions such as gambling, crime, food, sex, hoarding, debtors, and work are addressed in fellowships such as:

Clutterers Anonymous, (CLA) is a 12-step recovery programme which offers help to people who are overwhelmed by disorder in their lives. FAQs, literature, meeting list and CLA background information are available at: https://www.**clutterersanonymous**.org/

Debtors Anonymous (DA) helps people recover from compulsive debt and under-earning. **https://www.debtorsanonymous.org**

Emotions Anonymous is for recovery from mental and emotional illness and based on the 12-Steps of AA. **https://www. emotionsanonymous.org/**

Food Addicts in Recovery (FA) is a fellowship of men and women who have experienced difficulties in life as a result of the way they used to eat and were obsessed with food. They found they needed the 12-Step programme of recovery and fellowship of others who shared their problem in order to stop abusing food and begin living fulfilling lives: **https://www.foodaddicts.org**

Food Addicts Anonymous (FAA) Food Addicts Anonymous is an organisation that believes that food addiction is a biochemical disorder that occurs at a cellular level and, therefore, cannot be cured by willpower or therapy alone. We feel that food addiction is not a moral or character issue. This 12-Step programme believes that food addiction can be managed by abstaining from addictive foods, following a program of sound nutrition (a food plan) and working the Twelve Steps of the programme. After we have gone through a process of withdrawal from addictive foods many of us have experienced miraculous lifestyle changes. We are a fellowship of men and women who are willing to recover from the disease of food addiction. Sharing our experience, strength and hope with others allows us to recover from this disease One Day at a Time.

FAA is self-supporting through our own contributions. There are no dues or fees required for membership, but only a desire to stop eating addictive foods. We are not affiliated with any diet or weight loss programmes, treatment facilities or religious organisations. We neither endorse nor oppose any causes. Our primary purpose is to stay abstinent and help other food addicts to achieve abstinence. **https://www.foodaddictsanonymous.org/**

Gamblers Anonymous (GA) is a fellowship of men and women who share their experience, strength and hope with each other that they may solve their common problem and help others to recover from a gambling problem. The primary purpose is to stop gambling and to help other compulsive gamblers do the same. They are convinced that gamblers of their type are in the grip of a progressive illness. Over any considerable period of time, they get worse, never better.

The fellowship is the outgrowth of a chance meeting between two men in 1957. Both had a baffling history of trouble and misery due to an obsession with gambling. They began to meet regularly and, as the months passed, neither had returned to gambling. Since that time, the fellowship has grown steadily, and groups are flourishing in at least 58 countries in the world, many in local languages and dialects.

They concluded from their experience that, in order to prevent a relapse, it was necessary to bring about certain character changes within themselves. In order to accomplish this, they used for a guide certain spiritual principles that are today utilised by millions of people who are recovering from other compulsive addictions. The word spiritual can be said to describe those characteristics of the human mind that represent the highest and finest qualities such as kindness, generosity, honesty and humility. Also, in order to maintain their own abstinence, they felt that it was vitally important that they carry the message of hope to other compulsive gamblers. **https://www.gamblersanonymous.org.**

Gam-anon/Gam-ateen for friends and families of problem gamblers. **https://www.gam-anon.org/**

Homosexuals Anonymous (HA) to help people who want to live in freedom from homosexuality.

Neurotics Anonymous (NA) for recovery from mental and emotional illness. **https://www.recovery.org/support-groups/neurotics-anonymous/**

Overeaters Anonymous (OA) No matter what the problem with food – compulsive overeating, undereating, food addiction, anorexia, bulimia, binge eating or overexercising – OA has a solution: **https://oa.org/**

Parents Anonymous (PA) for parents who have abused children. **https://parentsanonymous.org/**

Racists Anonymous (RA) is a support group that deals with racism as almost a mental illness. **http://rainternational.org/**

Schizophrenics Anonymous for people effected by schizophrenia or bipolar disorder or psychotic depression. **http://www.sanonymous.org/**

Sexaholics Anonymous (SA) for people seeking recovery from sex addiction. **https://www.sa.org/**

Sex Addicts Anonymous (SA), is a 12-Step fellowship of recovering addicts that offers a message of hope to anyone who suffers from sex addiction. They are addicts who are powerless over their sexual thoughts and behaviours, and preoccupation with sex that was causing progressively severe adverse consequences for them, their families and friends. Despite many failed promises to ourselves and attempts to change, they discovered that they were unable to stop acting out sexually by themselves: **https://saa-recovery.org/**

Sex and Love Addicts Anonymous (SLAA) is a 12-Step programme for people recovering from sex addiction and love addiction. It is based on the model pioneered by Alcoholics Anonymous. **SLAA** is open to anyone who knows or thinks they have a problem with sex addiction, love addiction, romantic obsession, co-dependent relationships, fantasy addiction and/or sexual, social and emotional anorexia. If you have a desire to be free from Sex and Love addiction you may find it helpful to attend one of the meetings listed on the meeting list convenient for you. All meetings welcome newcomers. **www.slaauk.org/**

Sexual Compulsives Anonymous, (SCA) is a 12-Step fellowship, inclusive of all sexual orientations, open to anyone with a desire to recover from sexual compulsion. Our primary purpose is to stay sexually sober and to help others to achieve sexual sobriety. Members are encouraged to develop their own sexual recovery plan, and to define sexual sobriety for themselves. **www.sca-recovery.org/**

Survivors of Incest Anonymous (SIA) is a support group that helps people recover from childhood sexual abuse.

Sexual Recovery Anonymous (SRA) for those seeking recovery from sexual addiction.

Underearners Anonymous (UA) is for people who have difficulty providing for their needs, including those in the future. It is a 12-Step fellowship of people who have come together to help themselves and one another recover from underearning. It is not all of which are about money. While the most visible consequence is the inability to provide for one's needs, underearning is also about the inability to fully acknowledge and express our capabilities and competencies. It is about underachieving, or under-being, no matter how much money we make. The tools of UA include, and reinforce, the principles of recovery provided by the Twelve Steps. Members of UA also utilise additional tools – both individually and with partners – to support taking action that will create lives that are full, prosperous, and grounded in serenity. **https://www.underearnersanonymous.org/**

Workaholics Anonymous, (WA) is a fellowship of individuals who share their experience, strength and hope with each other that they may solve their common problems and help others to recover from workaholism. The only requirement for membership is the desire to stop working compulsively. www.**workaholics-anonymous**.org/

Auxiliary groups for friends and families of alcoholics and addicts, respectively, are part of a response to treating addiction as a disease that is enabled by family systems.

Al-Anon Family Groups

Al-Anon is a worldwide fellowship that offers a programme of recovery for the families and friends of alcoholics, whether or not the alcoholic recognises the existence of a drinking problem or seeks help.

Alateen is part of the Al-Anon fellowship, designed for the younger relatives and friends of alcoholics through the teen years.

Al-Anon and Alateen are fellowships of relatives and friends of alcoholics, who share their experience, strength and hope in order to solve their common problems. We believe alcoholism is a family illness and that changed attitudes can aid recovery. They are not allied with any sect, denomination, political entity, organisation or institution, do not engage in any controversy, neither endorses nor opposes any cause. There are no dues for membership. They are self-supporting through our own voluntary contributions.

Their groups have but one purpose: to help families of alcoholics. They do this by practising the Twelve Steps, by welcoming and giving comfort to families of alcoholics, and by giving understanding and encouragement to the alcoholic. The meetings often begin with the suggested Al-Anon/Alateen welcome, 'We welcome you to this Al-Anon Family Group and hope you will find in this fellowship the help and friendship we have been privileged to enjoy. We who live, or have lived, with the problem of alcoholism understand as perhaps few others can. We, too, were lonely and frustrated, but in Al-Anon and Alateen we discover that no situation is really hopeless, and that it is possible for us to find contentment, and even happiness, whether the alcoholic is still drinking or not.'

Al-Anon was co-founded in 1951, 16 years after the founding of Alcoholics Anonymous by Lois W (wife of AA co-founder Bill W) and Anne B.

Alateen began in California in 1957, when a teenager named Bob joined with five other young people who had been affected by the alcoholism of a family member.

Al-Anon and Alateen meetings are held in 56 countries, in local languages and dialects, as well as English. **https://al-anon.org/**

Families Anonymous (FA) is a 12-step fellowship for the family and friends of those individuals with drug, alcohol or related behavioral issues. **https://www.familiesanonymous.org/**

Adult Children of Alcoholics/Dysfunctional Families. (ACA) ACA's Twelve-Step programme was developed to deal with the effects of alcoholism or other family dysfunction found in such homes. The term 'adult child' was originally used to describe adults who grew up in alcoholic homes and who exhibited identifiable traits that reveal past abuse or neglect. Its members have histories of abuse, shame, co-dependency and abandonment found in dysfunctional homes. Today their groups include adults raised in homes without the presence of alcohol or drugs. Meetings are established in 50 countries and ACA literature is available in 19 languages. **www.adultchildren.org/**

Co-Dependents Anonymous (CoDA) addresses compulsions related to relationships. They have informal self-help groups made up of men and women with a common interest in working through the problems that co-dependency has caused in their lives. CoDA is based on the Alcoholics Anonymous Twelve Steps of recovery programme and adapted it to meet their purposes. To attend meetings, all you need is the willingness to work at having healthy relationships. This means that all kinds of people attend. Individual members can and do have differing political, religious, cultural, ethnic and other affiliations, but since these are not relevant to the business of recovery from co-dependency, no comment is made about them. CoDA has approximately 2,000 weekly meetings in 60 countries: there are also online and phone meetings. **www.coda.org/**

Co-Anon for friends and families of cocaine addicts.

COSA – groups for friends and families associated with Sex Addicts Anonymous.

Cosex and Love Addicts Anonymous (COSLAA) for friends and families with a sex or love addiction, associated with SLAA.

Gay and Sober https://www.gayandsober.org › This site will help you find an LGBT or LGBT friendly AA, NA, or CMA meeting in your area.

In addition, there are other closely patterned 12-Step fellowships established that cover different emotional and behavioral conditions. Details of these can be found on the internet or from medical professionals.

Definitions

Abstinence: the practice of restraint from indulging in something, typically alcohol, drugs, gambling, food or sex.

Addiction: addiction is a strong, uncontrollable need to take drugs, drink alcohol, smoke tobacco, gamble or carry out a particular activity. It becomes the most important thing in that person's life and leads to problems in relationships, at home, work and school. It seems there is no single reason why addictions develop.

Alcoholism: is a condition in which dependence on alcohol harms that person's health, family and social life, work and relationships.

Clean and sober is an expression used by drug addicts and alcoholics to define their condition, when their minds and bodies are free from **all** mood-altering drugs and alcohol.

Dependency: over-reliance on someone or something by a person similar or identical to the problems as those of addiction.

Drug addict is a person who is dependent on one or more mood-altering substances and whose life is usually wrecked as a result. There is usually a physical and psychological dependence.

Drug Users are not necessarily drug addicts. However, users should remember that prescription dependency creating medicines, alcohol, nicotine and caffeine are all drugs and can damage health, and when abused cause more damage to health and society than all the illegal drugs put together.

Harm Reduction: refers to policies, programmes and practices that aim to reduce the harms associated with the use of psychoactive drugs in people unable or unwilling to stop. The defining features are the focus on the prevention of harm, rather than on the prevention of drug use itself, and the focus on people who continue to use drugs. In other words, they do not cure addicts.

Narcotics are addictive drugs which are used to reduce mental or physical pain and often to induce feelings of euphoria. The word narcotic is derived from the Greek *narkotikos,* which means 'to numb' or 'deaden'; therefore, it can be applied to any drug, including alcohol or tranquillisers that causes this sensation.

Prescription Drug Addiction is the same as addiction to the **narcotics** described previously. The difference is these drugs are prescribed by medical professionals. Over time, users develop a tolerance leading to taking larger doses and addiction.